# The Writer's Friend

# The Writer's Friend*

*and a companion for copy editors and others who work with publications*

Martin L. Gibson

Iowa State University Press / Ames

Martin L. Gibson is Regents Professor of Communication, University of Texas at Austin.

Manufactured in the United States of America

First edition, 1989

### Library of Congress Cataloging-in-Publication Data

Gibson, Martin L., 1934–
    The writer's friend* : *and a companion for copy editors and others who work with publications /
Martin L. Red Gibson. – 1st ed.
        p.  cm.
    Includes index.
    **ISBN 0–8138–0149–4**
    1. Copy-reading.  2. Authorship.    I. Title.
PN162.G47  1989
    808′.02–dc19
                                                                        89-1774
                                                                            CIP

# Contents

# The Writer's Friend

# 1

# Writing Improvement

What we're trying to do here • 13 tips • 2 bigger tips

## What We're Trying to Do Here

I intend to help you learn to write better. We will use this book as a vehicle, and we will ride it to a new era of wealth, influence and public adulation. You will be acclaimed in world capitals and lionized at home. Women will throw themselves at your feet if you are a man. Men will throw themselves at your feet if you are a woman. But let's worry about literature now and think about sex later.

You can argue that we aren't aiming at literature in this book, that I stand closer to newspapers than to Nietzsche, closer to folklore than to Faulkner, closer to obits than to Ovid, and closer to stumpwater than to Shakespeare. Perhaps. However, newspaper people regularly attempt a kind of writing that others have not had to try, and I applaud them. First they have to gather and understand a set of facts. Then they have to arrange those in order of importance, judged objectively. Then they have to present these facts, no matter how arcane, in a manner that is readily understandable to most people but not offensively simplified to insiders. All this they do in hours, sometimes minutes.

They don't always do the job right.

But they try.

We will try, too, and we will look at writing in pieces and writing in a coherent whole. That means we will look at sentences and even individual words at times and will look at the complete work, as a unit, at other times.

Much of the material in this book got its start in columns written for *Publishers' Auxiliary* and the *Texas Press Messenger.* *Pub Aux,* a tabloid newspaper, is published for members of the National Newspaper Association; the *Messenger,* for the Texas Press Association. I rewrote much of this material to broaden its appeal. (The ideas apply to all kinds of writers, not just newspaper people, the primary audience.) I don't pretend everyone should write the way newspaper writers do. On the other hand, good newspaper writers write as well as anyone. They avoid jargon. They use metaphors and similes. They write with power, with grace, with humor. It's just that some of their subjects aren't suited for anything but a straightforward approach, such as we get with the five W's.

I'm trying to get newspaper writers to loosen up a little, though not to the point of giving us their feelings instead of the facts. They need to seem more human, more willing to realize that stories do not exist in a vacuum, with the lead decreed by providence. Newspaper people sometimes think the facts have arranged themselves and need merely to be plucked and put on paper by a passing reporter. Not so. Facts rarely come to us in the proper sequence. Someone must make a decision about importance. (You will not get a plea here for the abandonment of objective reporting; some people call it a myth, but I believe in trying for it.) Reporters make decisions for professional reasons, and then they try to tell stories to readers as they would to friends, possibly leaving out the strong language.

We will deal later with strong language and fancy language and other things that cause a deterioration of written communication.

You will find a lot of short sections in this book. In some of those, written as columns, I said all I wanted to say about a specific subject. This should work out all right, for it gives you a great range of subjects. You can find the revealed truth on a specific topic quickly, rather than having to search for it in a forest of other material. Of course, I hope you will wander through the whole forest; you may stumble upon some good stands of timber.

Some topics lend themselves to extra examination. I have included sentences from newspapers. I encourage you to go over them with a thought toward improving them. You will find further instructions nearer the offending sentences.

You need to think about improvements as you look at all writing. Choose the best way to express thoughts. I do not want to create a race of picky little pedants, running around and heaping ridicule upon people who do not know the difference between *comprise* and *compose.*

We're interested in improving communication, not showing up the ignorant. On the other hand, I would like to see every writer feel offended upon encountering slipshod writing. I would like to see every writer take a greater interest in the choices available in our language. I would like to see writers rejoicing over a pleasant turn of phrase, no matter whether they or someone else did the turning.

Francis Bacon had a pertinent thought: "Reading maketh a full man . . . " (Francis departed before sexual sensitivity reached us. If he were around today, he would surely recognize that women have achieved citizenship, and he would say reading maketh a full man or woman, or perhaps person.) "Reading maketh a full man, conference a ready man and writing an exact man." That means you have to read and gather some knowledge before you can offer wisdom or information to others. Next, you have to examine that knowledge from all sides—conference (we might call it debate). And then you have to present your knowledge in a precise way. You have to choose your words so the message the reader gets from your writing has about the same meaning you had in your own mind.

You cannot do this while watching TV game shows. Writing requires more discipline than some of us normally command. The microcomputer helps, because it lets us make changes in our work without getting crumpled sheets of paper all over the floor. Still, we have to be precise if we want to be called writers. We have to hang our words together, our sentences together, our stories together so readers stay with us and find and understand the information they want.

I commend you for your interest in this subject. The more you get into it, the more you will enjoy it. And if you improve yourself, even a little, we will all benefit.

# 13 Tips

Let's take a look at the sort of thing this book will handle. My first sermon against the sins of weak writing—you're reading it now—contains 14 paragraphs. Thirteen of them deal with problems and tips, just some ideas that an interested observer has gathered from a few years of looking at what people put into their newspapers. I offer them as commandments. They also look like topics to be expanded into 13 more sections in this book. However, not all get that treatment.

1. In a series, use the longest (or longer) item at the end. Not: *He was tired of playing second fiddle and eager.* Instead: *He was eager and*

*tired of playing second fiddle.* Not: *He liked long, leisurely strolls on the beach and mai tais.* Instead: *He liked mai tais and long, leisurely strolls on the beach.*

2. Eschew inordinately grandiloquent verbalization. Don't be fancy. Not: *The thieves gained entrance by breaking a door at the rear of the establishment.* Instead: *The thieves broke in through the back door.* Important point: You must filter this stuff out of the statements of people who talk this way. Most writing is helped by using quotations, but a writer must not just pump sewage right on through. Make the quotes into paraphrases or partial quotations without the fancy parts.

3. Watch out for all forms of *to be*. We have no weaker verb than *is*, which merely expresses existence. Not: *There is nothing that can ruin a sentence faster than a weak verb.* Instead: *Nothing can ruin a sentence faster than a weak verb.*

4. Get to the main verb. Verbs tell us what happened. They need to be near the front of the sentence or main informative clause. Not: *They said indigents, the wealthy, news reporters, doctors, editors, baseball players, cormorant lovers, truck drivers and midgets would get a free meal at the mission.* Instead: *They said the mission would have free Christmas dinners for indigents, the wealthy, news reporters,* etc.

5. Punctuate correctly. Newspaper writers could all benefit from a periodic re-examination of punctuation rules in an English handbook. Punctuation makes a great difference. Look back at No. 4. What happens if you drop the comma after *wealthy*? Right. You change the financial status of a lot of writing people. Punctuation helps the writer make precise statements. It helps readers understand precisely what the writer meant. We cannot have a better goal than that.

6. Beware of clutter. Go to the point. Strip out verbiage. Not: *A highway patrolman ran a routine check on the vehicle's license plates through the national computer, which revealed that the car, valued at $25,000, was stolen.* Instead: *A highway patrolman's routine license plate check showed that the $25,000 car was stolen.* Decide what will clearly be inferred by most readers. Most of that does not need to be included. We could assume, for instance, that a license check would involve a computer. We could assume that *$25,000* would refer to value, or at least to price; so we just call it a $25,000 car.

7. Be specific. Watch out for words like *several* and *may*. Not: *The board did several things last night to improve its financial position.* Instead: *The board took four steps to improve its financial condition last night.*

8. Get the modifier next to the clause it modifies. We're try-

ing to write with precision. Not: *Jones was driving the third car they saw from California.* Instead: *Jones was in the third car from California they saw,* or *Jones was in the third California car they saw.*

9. Beware of double verbs. Not: *He was attacked and mauled by a cougar.* Instead: *He was mauled by a cougar.* Not: *He got up and left.* Instead: *He left.* Not: *He was taken to the hospital and treated.* Instead: *He was treated at the hospital.* We can assume he was taken (not rushed, please) there or got there some way not requiring mention. If he was shot out of a cannon into the operating room, we could probably squeeze in a line or two on that. But a normal piece of transportation would require no notice in print.

10. Go easy on enhancers. Oh, I suppose we can occasionally get some mileage out of *somewhat, slightly, surely, totally* and perhaps even *very* and *real.* Well, maybe not *very.* But these and most others usually serve no purpose beyond protecting writers from the shock they get when they see they have made an unadorned statement.

11. Beware of unnecessary negatives. They confuse readers. Realize, too, that you can have a negative sentence without using *no* or *not* or *nor* and their kin. Example: *He disputed the players' statement that they were unable to turn down the arbiter's offer.*

12. Use quotations freely but carefully. You need them in most stories. Use them to enhance, to enliven, to explain. Do not use them to carry the narrative. For example, the listing of points in an itinerary can be done better in a paraphrase than in a quote. Example of explaining: *Bush said the plan would have worked if the news media had not revealed it prematurely. "When we lost the element of surprise, we lost everything," he told the visitors.*

13. Go from the general to the specific. Give us the big picture first. Tell us why the plane crashed before you give us the passenger list. Tell us someone's water well is contaminated first, and then you can tell us how much gunk has to be in the water before it is considered contaminated.

# 2 Bigger Tips

Let's try two more tips to improve your writing: 1. Get rid of comma clauses. 2. Use verbs instead of nouns.

Grammarians probably have a better term than *comma clause,* but that one suits me. You know it. Or at least you know one when you see it. Let me give you an example:

The governor had said that if all eight propositions had been approved, the state's income would be boosted by $6 billion.

We see that approach all the time. It usually comes about because we start down a path without seeing the end and we don't want to rewrite.

Commas slow the reader. Oh, I don't deny their value. We would be hard put to write clearly without commas. But they get in the way sometimes, as they do in the example, and the careful writer will not let them become impediments to understanding.

We avoid a comma in the sentence cited with this change: *The governor had said that approval of all eight propositions would increase the state's income by $6 billion.*

This version gives you a smoother read. You do not have the stop-and-start problem that commas sometimes give.

We have a marvelous language, and it provides a great amount of pleasure for writers who work at their craft. You can find comma clauses in your own writing. If you rewrite them, you will get better sentences. There's one now. Go back two sentences and rewrite it this way: *You will get better sentences if you rewrite them.*

You will find some sentences that need comma clauses. Such clauses allow you to shift the emphasis of a sentence. I would not think of making a flat rule against them. Use your sense. Revise when revision tightens your sentences.

Enough. Look at the other point. Consider replacing nouns with verbs. You cannot make this substitution all the time, of course. But you can make it often. And it almost always produces a better sentence. An example:

He used a chisel to take off half an inch of the stone beard.

Turn *chisel* into a verb and you get a better sentence: *He chiseled off half an inch of the stone beard.*

How about this one:

They asked him questions about his grandmother.

Sure. They questioned him.

Look at some more. I put verbs in parentheses after each sentence.

They showed signs of becoming a dominating force in the league. (signs of dominating the league)

He won abundant praise for taking a leadership role in the fight against censorship. (for leading)

She received resounding praise from both sides. (Both sides praised)

The doctor developed a specialty in hearing disorders after his internship. (specialized)

The court ruled that Smith committed libel against Jones with the article. (Smith's article libeled Jones)

She managed ascension of the stairs only with a great deal of trouble. (ascended)

They made her ashamed for trying the new makeup. (shamed her)

A crowd of nearly a thousand was in attendance. (attended)

He deposited all of his lottery winnings into the bank. (banked)

The British contingent had the tiny garrison under siege for two weeks. (besieged)

He took a bath every night. (bathed)

He made a quick calculation of their position. (quickly calculated)

The money came out of the box in a cascade. (cascaded from the box)

He was surprised that the people raised a clamor for him all day. (clamored)

She asked them to give the matter their consideration overnight. (consider it)

The creature was chased into a corner after an hour. (cornered)

He gave them a critique of their newspapers. (critiqued)

The shades made the room considerably darker. (darkened)

None of the visitors thought Taylor would engage in deception with them. (would deceive)

This opportunity for improving your copy comes up regularly. Learn to look for it and get better. Do it for your readers.

# 2

# Writing Requires Effort

Sentence length ● *Hooray for brevity. Let's make it readable.*
Clutter ● *Out with the useless. Words, sentences, paragraphs.*
Double-verbing ● Elegance ● *Somebody has to protect the language.*
*The ignorant go for false elegance.* Trimming the Fat ● *Chop, and don't*
*look back. The headless snake. The unfulfilled promise. The stricken color.*
Ellipsis: What's best left unsaid

In this chapter you get a bonus. Some sections have extra
sentences tagged on. You get to edit these. You can do the job with a
pencil (it's your book) or do them in your mind. I offer, in parentheses,
some thoughts about each sentence, but I encourage you to attack the
sentences on your own first. Decide how you would have written them.
Then check the parenthetical thoughts. If we disagree, be sure you
know why you like your way more than mine. Then stick with it; I
don't offer these answers as perfection. The better answer is the one
you choose. Mine will usually do the job.

Some other chapters—but not all—have the same approach.

## Sentence Length
### Hooray for Brevity

You have surely determined by now that I have in my body no
trace of pettiness. So I don't really get irritated when I reflect on the
extraordinary amount of money that Rudolph Flesch made with one
simple idea, an idea I could have had.

Mr. Flesch took a plain vanilla theory and gussied it up with some formulas and other bells and whistles. He offered it to the world as a readability measure, with a book, *The Art of Readable Writing,* as his medium.

His formulas boiled down to this: Short words are usually easier to understand than long words, and short sentences are usually easier to understand than long sentences.

Shucks, I could have told you that. So why did Flesch drive a Maserati and I drive a rusty Rabbit?

Actually, I don't know that Mr. Flesch drove a Maserati. But he should have. He deserved some reward for articulating a rather obvious observation about the writing racket. Get rid of his formulas and other things. Don't worry that a passage that scores 15.7 or 16.2 or whatever on his scale means no one but a doctor of literature will be comfortable with it. Just note the basic premise: Short sentences are usually easier to understand than long sentences.

We have other measures of readability. In one, called Cloze Procedure, researchers blank out a word every so often and see if readers can fill in the blank correctly. For example, in a story about a football coach's speech, we might encounter a statement that the coach wanted his team to "go out and kick a little blank tonight." Most people, especially people familiar with sports expressions, would be able to fill that in quickly. But if the blank fell in a statement like "The president will blank if the Russians don't quit," the percentage of correct guesses will dip. You get the idea: Readability scores fall in line with the number of blanks that people fill in correctly.

Cloze Procedure and the few dozen other readability measures are more sophisticated than the word-count method. But they require more time. And more effort. So I suggest you keep an eye on the number of words you use per sentence. *Time* magazine would like 20, I read somewhere once. (That's an admission I am not offering scholarly research here.) The Associated Press would be happy with 22.

I preach that you ought to start looking around for a place to stop as soon as you hit the third line on a typewriter. On the VDT a line commonly runs 80 characters (15 words). So I suggest you raise a warning flag for yourself as soon as you turn to the second line.

I once tried this idea on a group of PR people, and a Churchill fan in the crowd got agitated. He argued that Sir Winston wrote longer sentences than that and, by George, Winnie did all right in the literary world.

Well, yes. But you don't read *Their Finest Hour* while drinking your morning coffee and thinking about driving to work. You read

Churchill in a comfortable setting (I recommend it), usually with a good light and with no sense of urgency. Newspaper people, especially, write under different rules. Newspapers have to provide information in a form that readers can grab in a hurry. People can't—or won't—reread a paragraph they don't understand on the first pass. With Churchill, you sometimes reread a passage just for the pleasure of it, much as you commit long passages of this book to memory.

So I said those things to the PR man, wishing I had more ammunition to satisfy people who think writing isn't good unless it takes effort to read.

Then a brainstorm.

I got home and put the counter on Churchill. I mean, these people were telling me that Sir Winston was a great writer and did his work with mile-long sentences. I checked that out. And I checked Hemingway and Dostoyevski on the same trip, figuring that Ernest (in *The Old Man and the Sea*) would use shorter sentences than Churchill, and Fyodor would run longer. I expected Dostoyevski to go off the scale with long Russian sentences in *Crime and Punishment.*

Brace yourself for the results:

Churchill averaged 22.2 words per sentence. He ranged from two to 73, and 52 percent of his sentences had 20 words or fewer. Check that again. It says half his sentences had no more than 20 words each.

Hemingway averaged 13.5 words and had a range of three to 49. Eighty percent of his sentences had no more than 20 words.

Dostoyevski, the long-winded Russian, averaged 10.2 words, with a range of one to 29. Eighty-nine percent of his sentences had no more than 20 words.

I'm not pushing this as scientific. I picked three books I had at the house, chose the page number corresponding to my age, and started counting with the first complete sentence. I didn't get anything that would stand up in court, but I got a good indication that literature doesn't have to rely on mountainous sentences.

So, my advice: Try to hold most sentences to something like 20 words. Use a 30-worder now and then, for variety. Use some shorter ones. Beware always of those that go beyond 30 words; they ask too much from readers.

Sound reasonable? Good. Send the Maserati.

## Let's Make It Readable

The following sentences all throw the reader more information than can normally be digested at one sitting. Go through these, with a pencil or with an inquiring mind, and cut them into bite-size chunks.

With the state's budget crisis on everyone's mind, Allen Independent School District trustees spent most of Monday's meeting trying to save money as they discussed such usually routine items as driver's education, athletic equipment and roof warranties.

A period after *money* would begin to make this fit for human consumption.

Colonel Key High School is suffering from a lack of instructors to meet the needs of the students, according to Principal Jack Hinson, who made a request to the Board of Education Monday night that a new position for a combination math/science teacher be considered.

You cannot save this one with punctuation. Maybe: *Colonel Key High School should create and fill a math and science teaching job, the principal said Monday.*

If the enrollment doesn't increase for the two agriculture courses and the evening adult program offered at the Spring Vocational School, the Spring Board of Education may be faced with the decision that it will have to phase out those offerings effective next year.

Try this: *Lack of enrollment threatens to kill two agriculture courses and the evening adult program at Spring Vocational School.*

Sophomore tailback Techie Verdun rushed for 123 yards and scored two touchdowns, senior quarterback Jim Kratatoa passed for 211 yards and one TD and wide receiver Cris Oleay hauled in seven passes for 103 yards and a six-pointer as Wobegon State defeated Northeastern 30-9 before 89,808 in Big Eleven football action at Juggo Stadium on an overcast but warm November Saturday afternoon.

Too much. You have to give us the broad version, the generic picture, before slapping on the details. Try: *Techie Verdun, Jim Kratatoa and Cris Oleay led Wobegon State to a 30-9 victory over Northeastern here Saturday.* You can tell us how they did their leading later.

The cotton harvest in many counties in the Alberta highlands was at or near a complete standstill as of Wednesday from the weekend storms and ensuing rains, while a fortunate few were able to be spared from the damaging weather and were able to continue with harvest on a day-to-day basis.

Call a halt after *rains.* Then give us much of the rest in a second sentence.

If you are a dog lover and appreciate the performance of a disciplined animal, trained to perfection and ready to do that for which he has been bred, you will take pleasure in observing the All-America Foxhunters Field Trial Association events scheduled to begin today at the Coldwater Recreational Facility Area in the Blackwater River State Forest near Munson, where some of the best hounds in the nation will be running red or gray foxes in closely judged competition.

Someone actually ran that in a newspaper. Well, I doctored it to disguise the location, but I didn't make it up or add words. It requires complete rewriting. I have no particular objection to using all that stuff, though it sounds a little flowery; but we cannot use it all in the lead. Some must go in later sentences or paragraphs.

# Clutter
## Out with the Useless

You can keep a lot of your sentences down to a reasonable length with some careful trimming, and with a little thought. Practice helps. You need to get the habit of eliminating excess baggage in your prose. If you learn to delete it when you see it, soon you will learn to avoid it as you write.

You call this problem useless wording, I call it clutter, and the fancy people call it verbiage. By any name, it has to be rooted out of our writing if we expect to communicate with our readers.

I'm talking about words whose job is already handled by other words in a sentence. Example: *Inspectors searched for a missing thumb-size cylinder containing radioactive material.* No one ever searched for something that wasn't missing. Since the word *search* covers this idea, we can kill *missing* as clutter.

## Words, Sentences, Paragraphs

Is a saving of one word worth the effort? Sure. Moreover, the idea counts more than the saving of words. First you get in the habit of deleting useless single words, and then you can work your way up to extra clauses, extra sentences and even redundant paragraphs.

Let me hit you with two paragraphs, and you mentally edit for clutter. Say you are editing for a Texas newspaper (that's important this time):

> Houston was the leading city in the state of Texas in the number of murders recorded last year, according to FBI information released this morning.
>
> The information was put forth by the FBI in its quarterly Uniform Crime Reports. Houston was listed in first place in Texas and third in the nation in the number of murders committed, with 716 murdered in the period covered by the FBI report.

All right. Obviously Houston is a city and Texas a state. So we rephrase the first part to use a strong verb: *Houston led the state in murders last year.* . . . (Remember, this was for Texas newspapers; that makes use of *the state* acceptable.) Next, how do people keep track? They count, with numbers; so Houston just led in murders, not *the number of* murders. You can also make a case for dropping *recorded,* since no one leads in unrecorded murders.

That brings us to the attribution. Strip out the clutter (*according to FBI information released this morning*) and say *the FBI reported today.* That gives us a little more life, too.

Now comes the best part of this sermon. Convert the first sentence in the second paragraph into something tighter that covers the material of two sentences. Say this:

> The FBI's quarterly Uniform Crime Reports also listed Houston third in the nation with 716 murders for the year.

As before, you do not need to refer to *the number of murders,* because that is the only way we count. If we say *for the year* at the end, we can drop the longer clause *in the period covered by the FBI report.* Actually, we could eliminate *for the year,* because the lead indicated the time covered.

We have said precisely as much as before, but we have done it in 31 – or 28 – words instead of the original 69.

You will not be able to make such a wholesale saving every day, even if you work on a newspaper copy desk; reporters at your place will seldom shower you with as many errors as seen here. However, you will get those lapses, and others, in dribbles. You will see some of them in your own copy and more in others' copy. Dig them out.

Look at a few doubled clauses from fairly recent newspaper stories:

> . . . a *unanimous* 92-0 vote.
> . . . he is *a man who is* competent.
> . . . in medicine as well as *the field of* philosophy.
> . . . he had not had *enough* time to study the record.
> . . . skidded 25 feet and *came to a stop* (stopped).

Let's do a few more, first with the cluttered version and then, in parentheses, something better. Do not accept my version as gospel; try to improve on it, too.

> The two planes collided at a height of 8,000 feet above the Grand Canyon. (The planes collided 8,000 feet above the Grand Canyon.)
>
> There is nothing that can devastate a budget faster than illness. (Nothing can devastate a budget faster than illness.)
>
> He was afraid the period of the truce would be misused. (He was afraid the truce would be misused.)
>
> If a customer in the restaurant doesn't leave the waitress a tip, Jones takes 10 percent of the check and gives it to her. (If a diner leaves no tip, Jones gives the waitress 10 percent of the check.)
>
> The House promised to take all necessary measures to see that tax breaks would be spread evenly. (The House promised to spread tax breaks evenly.)
>
> The dean said all students who are interested in participating in the tryouts were urged to be there at 9 a.m. Monday morning. (The dean said students who want to try out should be there at 9 a.m. Monday.)

Terms like *who are* (as in *who are interested*) can often come out with no pain. Similarly, we get rid of some verbiage by having people try out instead of participating in tryouts. Now then, if we really want to use the blowtorch, we can legitimately go with something like this: *Tryouts begin at 9 a.m. Monday.* This approach gets the news columns out of the advertising business. It does not belittle tryouts or deans, but it makes a statement and lets readers choose to try out without our active suggestion.

You will not comb all the clutter from your prose, but you can take care of some of it with a little attention. Go over your own work, just as I will go over this in print. Fix the bad parts and resolve not to let verbiage, clutter or useless wording get into your copy next time.

# Double-verbing

OK, so you can't make a verb out of *verb.* Let's worry less about that than about the problem it covers: the use of two predicates when one will do. This problem, which I call double-verbing, should have disappeared as more and more people grew accustomed to word processors. But it stays with us. A mystery. With the word processor (newspaper people call theirs *terminals* or *screens* or *VDTs*), a writer should be able to tighten his or her work much easier than with a typewriter. We have to put out less effort.

Unfortunately, some of us reduce our effort even more — we don't exert any at all when working on our own material. Thus we err. We transgress. We never develop the attitude that forces us to weigh every sentence. We don't develop the sense of shame we should have after producing, or passing, a miserable sentence. We don't care.

We find ourselves guilty of double-verbing and don't bother to thin out the extra word. This bit of mental slackness causes us to say someone is taken to the hospital and treated. We need say only that our victim was treated at the hospital; readers can infer that he got there some normal way. If he went in a dogsled or other peculiar conveyance (a cannon was mentioned in the previous chapter), we would certainly cite the transportation. Otherwise, we waste reader time.

The same thing goes with sentences saying someone got up and left. Oh, someone in a wheelchair could leave without getting up, I suppose. And if you spend much time in seedy bars, you will probably see someone dragged out by the leg without having to get up. But generally speaking, getting up precedes leaving. That's automatic. You waste reader time by mentioning it.

If we cared about our writing, if we went back over it, we would not produce sentences like the following, all from reputable newspapers.

The Marines on the line are using an old oil drum to wash their clothes in.

Don't worry about the preposition on the end. Concentrate on the double-verbing. Just say: *The Marines wash their clothes in an old drum.* Cut through the underbrush. Help your readers.

The original atrium plan did not comply with the code because it exceeded the density limits and didn't include loading spaces, Ballard said.

We need only one verb. Let *exceeded* carry the idea of *did not comply.* Thus: *The original atrium plan exceeded the code's density limits and did not include required loading spaces, Ballard said.*

The St. Lucie County grand jury won't issue a report on its findings before election day.

Just say it won't report on its findings before election day. Use *report* as a verb and let it carry the idea of a noun, too. This book does not contain a sentence more important than the one just before this.

Firemen say that the fire which broke out in uptown Galion Thursday morning caused about $80,000 in damage.

We could get a week's grammar lessons out of that one. First, strengthen the sentence by putting the facts before the attribution. Then change your *which* to *that* because you have a restrictive clause: *the fire that broke out.* Then delete the clause you have just fixed. You don't need it; if a fire did $80,000 worth of damage, we can assume it broke out. Therefore: *Thursday's fire in uptown Galion caused about $80,000 in damages, firefighters said.*

To review the damage which has occurred on roads and bridges. . . .

What does damage do besides occur? Not much. So: *To review the damage to roads and bridges.* . . .

Jonathan was seriously injured when their van was struck and knocked over by a car.

If the van was knocked over, surely it was struck. Use only one verb.

That only caused his rage to intensify.

Say it intensified his rage.

Licensed alligator hunter Tom Gore lassoed the critter and took it to the savannas, where it was released.

We can figure out that if he released it there, he got it out there somehow. We need not say he took it *and* released it. Now, if he saddled it and rode to the savannas at a high gallop, that would be worth mentioning. But an ordinary bit of transportation need not take up space or reader time.

A year ago Mayville State came to Huron and later departed with a win.

Two problems. First, we throw in a useless verb. Readers know Mayville State has to come to town before Mayville State can leave. We don't need to say that. Second, the original sentence emphasizes the comings and goings. We want to focus instead on the action, the winning. So we do this: *Mayville State won last year's game in Huron, 19-0.*

When deputies drove to the airport, they found the car right off.

That construction makes the trip more important than the finding. Say deputies quickly found the car at the airport; we can infer they drove there or got there some other unimportant way.

Projecting the hissing sound of a snake, the owl communicated its fear to the curious audience.

Instead: *Hissing like a snake, the owl. . . .*

Jack Brown, a pharmacist, appeared before the City Council Thursday and complained about an inability to get his business garbage picked up.

As always, we can save time by eliminating parts the reader will automatically infer. Tell us that Jack complained to the city council; we readers will assume he appeared. If he complains in a letter or a telephone call—neither an ordinary path—the story must say so. Could we tighten this more? Possibly. We could say he complained about poor garbage collection at his business. We would do better to specify the nature of poorness—noisy, sporadic, late or whatever. Finally, if we mentioned the pickup at *his pharmacy,* we would not have to call him a pharmacist earlier.

You can find a pile of similar examples with any amount of searching at all. Start looking in your own copy. The word processor will help you in the revision, the correction, the improvement. It won't help in the search; you have to spot the problems and make the corrections, in your copy or someone else's. You have to do the work. You have to work until it's time to get up and leave.

# Elegance
## Somebody Has to Protect the Language

Elegance of design delights us. Elegance of thought lifts us. Elegance of language inspires us.

And false elegance exposes us as amateurs.

False elegance—inflated writing, elevated language, unnecessarily fancy wording—can be fatal in communication. We do ourselves in, and not for good reason.

Too many writers go overboard in reaching for elegance of style. They grab instead a fistful of false elegance, the sign of an amateur or at best a hack. These people abound. I'm raising a guerrilla force to root them out. You can join the team if you care enough to work at preservation of writing quality.

The language is in enough trouble without professional writers adding to the abuse. We can forgive the ignorant for not knowing about their language. (We forgive them, but we also encourage them to take up some other line of work.) We cannot forgive the thoughtless rascals who abuse the language by reaching for the elevated word at every opportunity. We cannot forgive the speaker who thinks the meat of his bland prose requires the ketchup of polysyllabic adjectives.

We are not discussing Churchill here. We're criticizing people who purchase something instead of buying it, people who articulate concepts instead of telling about ideas.

Some of these people make a living as news writers. However, news writers rank only third or fourth among offenders when it comes to abuse of the language. Government people are the worst. Then comes the public relations crowd. After that, we have newspaper writers and academicians.

Academicians started life as schoolteachers. Then they got puffed up enough to become educators. When the novelty of that title wore off, they climbed one more peak and became academicians. We will have to call them knowledge enhancement specialists before long.

I do not say you cannot use language to fool the people. I just say you ought to be ashamed of yourself if you do, on purpose or not. Elegance of language has no value if not accompanied by elegance of thought.

We see false elegance most often among the insecure. They confuse fanciness with importance and dress up mental mediocrity in linguistic finery. They fear that a normal vocabulary will not impress people. They cannot say they know someone 37 years old; that person has to be 37 years of age. They cannot say someone got a new job; they say he or she secured new employment—or has elected to pursue a new career opportunity.

The problem worsens as the disease feeds off itself. An insecure official who sees another insecure official quoted in the newspaper—TV is worse—thinks people are *supposed* to talk that way. The logic: "If a person is smart enough or important enough to be quoted in the news, that person must be good with the language. Therefore, to be important I must talk that way." They do not put their thoughts into precisely those words, but that's the idea. People talk like others they see quoted.

We pick up cues from strange sources. Walking from the arena after a basketball game, I heard a fellow say to a friend: "Boy, they were putting it to us until we reeled off those 12 unanswered points there at the end."

That poor lad had been contaminated by sportswriters. I wanted to look up a sportswriter and give him 12 unanswered whacks on the ear for leading the innocent astray.

Don't get me wrong. I'm not pushing a return to "See Spot. See Spot run. See Spot do it on the carpet."

Hardly.

I'm just complaining about the conversion of all our TV writers into media critics. I dislike the metamorphosis of typists into information processors. I don't mind the use of a word like *metamorphosis* if that word fits just right. But I hate to see good janitors turned into custodial engineers because someone thinks janitors would be better citizens if we pumped up the title.

Let's look at some more cases.

Take Bill Clements, twice elected governor of Texas. As governor, he was quoted daily in the newspapers. Once he said the federal voting rights act "prohibits a retrogression in the position of racial minorities in respect to their effective exercise of the electoral franchise."

A pity. Governors do not have to talk like that. They can say, as Clements should have said, that the voting rights act says you cannot do anything to keep blacks and Hispanics from voting as much this year as they did last year.

Clements went the long way around, and newspapers slavishly quoted him.

Take Linda Ronstadt. She had the best version of the song "Blue Bayou" some years ago. Note the words carefully: *I'm going back someday, come what may, to Blue Bayou, where the fishing boats, with their sails afloat, if I could only see a familiar sunrise, through sleepy eyes, how happy I'd be.*

The late Roy Orbison, who wrote that song, grew up in a dry part of the country. He did not know that if your fishing boat has its sails afloat you will be slow getting home that night. We can overlook that lapse; we have a bigger target. When Linda gets to the passage about boats, she sets us up for a verb: *where the fishing boats, with their sails afloat*—VERB, Linda. *Do* something. We cry for a verb, and we get only a familiar sunrise.

We're in the twilight of precise use of the language.

I hate to sound so crabby in this discussion of the arts, but someone has to speak sharply to these entertainers who take the language down with them as they sink into the depths of semiliteracy.

Less newsworthy people are just as bad. A school board member was recently quoted as telling teachers not to ask for more money because the board was in a zero increase posture. A hospital referred to negative patient outcome, meaning the patient died. The New Jersey Crime Commission talked about "members of a career offender cartel," namely the Mafia.

Another burst of nonsense from academicians referred to "enhancement of peer group interaction skills." That means they were going to try to teach kids to get along better with playmates.

We have somehow let the government and the schoolteachers—I mean the educators, no, I mean the academicians . . . we have let these people give us impactful news instead of news with impact. We let advertisers give us products with stimulative functions, instead of stimulating products. We see basketball players scoring at the end of fast break opportunities, instead of scoring on fast breaks. Instead of having to punt, football teams face punting situations. We let all kinds of people give us major breakthroughs (no simple minor breakthroughs) as we prioritize our concepts.

I read a PR release noting a period of continuing unprofitability. The person who wrote that did not want to risk being fired for telling the world the company was still losing money.

A government official reportedly once said, "We were not micromanaging Grenada, intelligence-wise, until about that time frame."

Another abuse: We turn the language sideways with strange participles. Walking down a hotel corridor, I saw a sign: *Warning. Do not open. These doors are alarmed.* I assumed the windows were terrified. I hardly slept a wink that night, figuring a hotel that would be so careless with the language would surely be lax in protecting guests from thieves and arsonists.

A newspaper ad for condos overlooking Central Park noted that they had windowed kitchens.

We have other sinners. None are bad enough to lose sleep over, but they indicate the breadth of the problem. I have seen these things in newspapers:

> hourly pay annualized
> ships homeported
> an island condoed
> employees badged and medicalized
> a company medicalized
> tomato sauce jarred
> grocery items couponed
> a valley sewered

Some of those things will get into the language, and I do not truly object. We will all talk about digitized information someday. *Formalized* has made it, though many of us dislike the word. The language changes, with new words being added all the time. We should have one rule of thumb, however: Do not get out front in the parade celebrating a new word. Let other people bring it into the language. If the word catches on, you will have plenty of time to use it. Indeed, you do not want to lag so far behind that you seem old-fashioned.

You will know when the time has come. You know we no longer boggle at seeing something finalized, but we have not quite become accustomed to having an intersection signalized.

And now the point of today's sermon: If you write or edit a piece of copy containing false elegance, no matter what the source, you sin if you let it pass. (Sometimes, when showing the flavor of a person, you quote fancy or, more likely, ungrammatical passages. That topic is treated later in the book.) Your job, as a carrier of information, requires you to knock off the quotation marks and put the offending speaker's words into understandable English. This means work. You have to understand the story yourself. You cannot take the lazy way out, throwing readers a quotation they have to decipher. You cannot endanger the rest of us merely by using someone else's tortured syntax. You cannot wash your hands and claim that you are only a reporter.

Good writers do not abuse the language, and they do not let anyone abuse it through them.

## The Ignorant Go for False Elegance

I'm not sure we have exorcised the elegance demon. It will thrive as long as writers are afflicted by a desire to impress, compounded by long exposure to the attitude that we ought to write a little better than we talk.

Truth is, we should. When writing, we can pause for days while we work on the way we want to put something. We don't have any *ers* and *ahs,* any *you knows* and so on. We don't have inflections and raised eyebrows or smirks, so we need to be a little more formal than we are in speech.

But that doesn't mean we have to use fancy words when plainer, more easily understood words lie close at hand. I am referring to the habit of using such things as *prior to* instead of *before.*

Maybe I'm being contradictory. Maybe I'm trying to have my elegance and forbid it, too. And then again maybe I'm trying to say that you have to do some line-drawing of your own in this area. You have to define slipshod use of the language, including slang, and distinguish that from merely an informal, personal style.

After you decide, let me encourage you to have second thoughts before you use words like those we're going to check now.

*Prior to* . . . You always say *before* in writing a letter or talking to people. Why do you change for your newswriting?

*Purchase* . . . I can see using this word now and then as a noun, but *buy* does a much better job as a verb.

*Attorneys* . . . I call them *lawyers.*

*Concept* . . . An *idea* with delusions.

*Transported* . . . This is the ambulance drivers' favorite. This is what they say when they mean they took the guy to the hospital.

*Experiencing difficulty* . . . Someone's having trouble.

*Electronic media* . . . Turn on the radio or television.

*Is in violation of* . . . We use this construction too often. Business people say they are in receipt of a communication, when they mean they got the letter. The phrase got into my list from a newspaper that said some policy was in violation of the law. Yes, that's understandable. But why couldn't we say it's against the law or it violates the law? We could.

*Comprise* . . . First, this word is misused at least as often as it is used correctly. It is not a synonym for *compose,* though a lot of people are trying to make it one. The whole comprises the parts. The team comprises 11 players. His work comprises prose, poetry and music. I wouldn't kid you. We err by raising our elegance level a notch and abandoning *compose. Comprise* is longer and more exotic, so we think we ought to use it. Stick with *compose* and *make up* when you tell us how many players a team has.

*Subsequent to* . . . You mean *later* or *after,* depending on the sentence.

*Interact* . . . The academicians (schoolteachers, remember) gave us this one. It has many meanings, from *get along* to *affect each other.*

I won't go so far as to say you are an evil person if you use some of these words now and then. We all slip over the line of needless elegance. All that I ask is that you recognize when you are using these terms and others that you would seldom use in conversation. Nothing looks sillier than an egregiously inappropriate manifestation of an inordinate desire to effect the implementation of polysyllabic terminology.

I fell into the company of a bunch of wordsmiths the other night at a local refreshment stand, and the topic turned to redundant words. Let me offer you our list. You know where to reach me if you want to add to it. Please do.

| | |
|---|---|
| 12 noon | first began |
| eyewitness | sworn affidavits |
| totally destroyed | hot-water heater |
| basic fundamentals | free gift[1] |
| bald-headed | widow woman |

---

1. An atlas company once promised me a "complimentary free gift" just for bringing in a card.

| | |
|---|---|
| current trend | old adage |
| at the intersection of | old traditions |
| violent explosion | invited guests |
| Easter Sunday | major breakthrough |
| repeat again | Jewish rabbi |
| fellow classmates | large-sized |

I'm sure we had more, but I have forgotten them in the excitement.

# Trimming the Fat
## Chop, and Don't Look Back

If you work for a news organization, you will soon realize you end your workday with more knowledge than you have imparted to readers.

Don't worry about it.

Your job requires that you give readers the gist of all stories they want and need. It requires that you provide enough information for readers to make necessary decisions. It does not require that you supply all possible details on every story you run.

If you edit for a living—your own copy or someone else's—you must learn to chop fearlessly, to cut out duplication, to eliminate the inconsequential. And you must do the work on your own material as well as that from the farthest outposts covered by a wire service.

We call this work trimming, and many of us do it inadequately. Let's look.

A story from an Ohio newspaper that reached my desk told about a police chase involving a stolen car. The reporter did not know how to compress this information, so he simply reeled off the story chronologically. As a result, we got a sentence about every twist and turn of the chase. We got all the highway numbers and directions and names of lawmen involved. We did not need that much information. We needed to know only that a 12-minute, 12-mile chase involved police, highway patrolmen and sheriff's deputies from three counties.

There you have the reporter's job. Reporters get paid to assimilate information, to sift out its importance, and then to compress it into an easily swallowed pill of information. If the car chase goes through downtown, we need to say that. But we don't need to enumerate the back roads.

Writers and editors also need to tighten stories by collapsing, which you may refer to as compressing. Here's an example of two sentences that can be collapsed into one: *The school board said it would like to have bids on both buildings. If no one wanted both, trustees indicated, bids on just one would be considered.* Collapse that to this: *The school board wanted bids on one or both of the buildings—preferably both.*

Don't follow this advice out the window. If you turn two sentences into one extra-long sentence, you have erred. You're better with two of about 20 words each than one of 35. Don't sacrifice understanding for brevity, especially if you don't really get brevity.

Trimming includes other problems. Look at three: the headless snake, the unfulfilled promise, and the stricken color.

## The Headless Snake

You often see the snake in identification. You are reading along and you run into some fellow's last name, some name you do not remember. This can happen when an editor deletes a paragraph that contains the first name. Then the editor does not notice that the last name stands alone now.

This sentence showed up in the middle of a weather report: *The other storm hit East Texas before daylight.* Fine, but the story had not mentioned a first storm. I suspect an editor took out one paragraph or more in the middle, getting rid of the first storm, because it was in another state.

Editors and writers make this mistake because they have the information in their minds but don't get it onto their pages or their VDT screens. Readers read sentences, not minds.

## The Unfulfilled Promise

The same Ohio story about the car chase said: *The victim carried no identification, but a woman's identification was found in the car.* And we heard no more on that. I checked this one out. The police had called the woman and thus found out the man's name. Unfortunately, that fact did not show up in the paper. Readers judge us on what we print, not what we keep to ourselves. Don't flood readers with every detail, but provide enough to make the story whole.

Another story ended this way: *It was not the first time the rules have come into play in major championships. The most famous case was Roberto de Vicenzo of Argentina, who birdied the 17th hole at Augusta during the final round of the 1968 Masters and, apparently, tied Bob Goalby at the end of the regulation 72 holes, setting up a play-off.* End of story. Start of mystery.

That came from carelessness. The story ran too long, and someone clipped it off without reading. All of us know better.

The problem is not confined to newspapers and other professional publications. It can occur in letters and office memos. It happens because we do not pay attention to what we have put on paper. We writers know exactly what we mean, but our meaning isn't necessarily what someone else will think upon seeing our words.

## The Stricken Color

Too many hard-bitten desk denizens automatically scratch the quotation or the little flair in a piece of writing when they have to make a trim. They often err. Editors should not take the color out of writing. Stifle gaudy ornamentation, yes; color, no. A good pithy quote that will keep readers with the story can be of more value than some facts. Not all facts. But some. Don't strike the color as a reflex action. If it does more for the story than a fact would, save it.

Trim thoroughly, deeply and fearlessly. But do it with some care.

# Ellipsis: What's Best Left Unsaid

Good use of the language lies somewhere between Pidgin English ("him fella go town") and the police report ("the suspect individual did at that time endeavor to transport himself to the alleged town"). Agreed, you have to be specific, so people can understand your precise meaning. But you need not overload your sentences, your comments, your thoughts, with useless wording.

Some words are like jalapeño peppers; you can take them away, but the flavor, or in this case the meaning, lingers behind. We call that ellipsis. The reader grasps the missing word's meaning, just as the heat of a jalapeño remains with you for a while.

Example: *I met three men last night. Two were Canadians.* You do not need to say two *of the men* were Canadians. A reasonable person would see that at once. The words leave their meaning even though we have deleted them.

But fearful journalists sometimes overlook the value of ellipsis. They take the police-report approach and throw in the extra words, rather than run the risk. (Actually, they see a risk where none exists.) Let's look at some sentences that need help.

> The site, which is located northwest of Dallas, is favored by the FCC.

That has a lot of waste. Start by scrapping *which is.* That takes away nothing important. *Which is* is clearly understood. Keep going. Take out *located.* You have still lost nothing, except three words. We have not approached pidgin; we have just eliminated some useless wording. Try another:

> TCU still has its home-court winning streak, which at 22 games is the fourth-longest current Division I home winning streak. Kansas heads the Division I list with a current 45-game home winning streak.

That mess, straight from a newspaper, shows a great deal of uncertainty in the writer. The first clause tells us what kind of streak TCU has. We do not need to repeat ourselves. We should have this as our first sentence: *TCU still has a 22-game home-court winning streak, fourth longest in Division I.*

All right, our first sentence tells about streaks and number of games. So the next sentence need not say again that we are referring to home games or, indeed, even to games. Furthermore, our single reference to Division I will do nicely. Instead of spelling out all the facts, we should use wording that allows readers to fill in any blanks. We can thus get by with two fairly short sentences by adding: *Kansas leads with 45.*

Another:

> The Redmen made good on 22 of 44 field goal attempts. The Hoyas managed only 18 of 47 field goal attempts.

Surely you see the need to kill the last three words. The writer did not. He was afraid people would think the Hoyas managed only 18 of 47 free throws, or 18 of 47 passes, or something. The writer erred; no literate person would misunderstand the second sentence if we ended at *of 47.* We offend people, not to mention slowing them down, with the extra words.

Every editing textbook has a sentence saying two cars collided at *the intersection of* Main Street and Central Avenue. Students are supposed to delete the offending words. Usually they do. They see the offense quickly, or certainly after it has been pointed out once, and you would think this little error would disappear. It doesn't. It stays with us, sometimes disguised as *at the corner of.* When we get in a hurry, we sometimes let these things go by. But if we practice eliminating them while unhurried, we can take them out automatically (if we're lucky, we and other writers will never put them in), no matter how near the deadline.

One more:

> Gastonians Burl Vise, Ed Long and Wang Kung have been found innocent in their trial on charges of disseminating obscenity. The jury reached its verdict in the three-day trial early Tuesday afternoon. The three were on trial for the second time on the disseminating obscenities charges.

We could collapse that a number of ways, but for the moment let us concentrate on the repetition. We have no reason at all to repeat the nature of the charge. Readers easily remember the charge, especially with no other kind of charge mentioned to throw them off. If we had other charges or distractions, we could help readers with the repetition. Since we do not, we should kill the useless words.

I'm too lazy to make up a list of offending words, but common sense will contribute to any list you put together. For example, no one leads in unreported crimes. A story about crime statistics is obviously built around items reported. We have unreported crimes, no doubt, but by definition they are not being counted. Similarly, if one person weighs 185 pounds, the second person in that sentence or even paragraph can just weigh 190; we understand *pounds.* If one player scores 20 points in the first half, we can say, for example, that an opponent had 15; we do not need to say the opponent had 15 *points* or, worse, 15 points in the same period.

That gets us to headlines. We use ellipsis in headlines. For example: *2 dead in U.S. 90 crash.* Readers know we do not mean two cows or two birds. No problem. But now a warning: We can go overboard here, as we can in body type. If people misunderstand us because we shorten our sentences, we err. Better to put in extra wording than be misunderstood. That's why I enjoy the following headline from my old files:

**Blizzard hits 3 states; 1 missing.**

# 3

# Some Work with Words

Some playful words • *How about that zeugma? Metaphors: a breath of fresh air.* The weakest verb • *It is is, isn't it? Get rid of it.* *Which* and *that* • Sexist pronouns: he/she said to him or her • Dangling dangers: when reading, these can fool you • Cliches: they're as thick as hops • Contractions: don't be afraid of them

## Some Playful Words

This chapter contains a mixture of things. You will enjoy some lightheartedness in a couple of the items, though they have serious intent behind them. Let's start with some unusual words.

### How About That *Zeugma?*

*Ecdemolagnia* means "the tendency to be more lustful when away from home."

Or at least that's what Rena Pederson of the *Dallas Morning News* says it means. She got the definition from Charles Osgood, the TV fellow who sometimes talks in rhyme. He got it from some dictionary bigger than any of mine. Or he made it up.

Either way, it set Rena off on a jaunt through the newsroom, collecting favorite words of staffers. Paula La Rocque used Rena's report in her monthly *F.Y.I.* critique sheet for the *News*.

Osgood also likes *gyromancy,* "the art of prophesying by spinning around in circles so fast you fall down." Osgood, in a Dallas speech, noted, "We do that at CBS News, but we call it 'instant analysis.'"

Rena offered as her personal favorite *borborygmus,* which most of us know as the gut-rumbles. I prefer the plural, *borborygmi,* but who's picky?

An editorial writer chose *kakistocracy,* which is defined as "government by the worst people." That has a suspicious look, as if someone had started with *kaka* and worked backward. But the big *Webster's* lists it.

*News* staffers chose words a cut above those you usually see on lists like this. To tell the truth, you don't usually see lists like this. Listmakers prefer to collect words someone considers the loveliest in the language. You get words like *mellifluous, luminescent* and *sensuous.* These words, though usable, depend in part on connotation, on mental pictures, for their attractiveness.

Those from the *News* rely more on definition.

Take one from still another editorial writer (the *News* has a platoon of them): *cacophony,* "a discordant sound." Also, editorial page editor Jim Wright likes *tintinnabulation,* "a ringing or tinkling of bells." *Mafficking* strikes me as a superior offering, though its nominator complained that he can't get headline writers to use it on a story about the OU-Texas football weekend. It means "boisterous celebration, as in making a fool of yourself in the streets," Rena says.

The next time you're looking for a word to tell about a movement within a part of a country that had been part of another country and wants to return to the original country, try *irredentism,* a favorite of *Texas Almanac* editor Mike Kingston. Mike would know about that sort of thing.

Others: *Eschew,* "to avoid or forgo"; *concatenation,* "a linked series of events"; *osculate,* "to kiss"; *discombobulate,* "to upset someone's composure"; *meiotic,* "having to do with understatement"; *abulia,* "the loss of the ability to make decisions"; and *chrematophobia,* "the fear of money."

Rena gave her prize to a drama critic for *diseuse,* "a skilled and usually professional woman reciter, a woman who recites verse or other text to music."

I would have supported *zeugma,* a figure of speech in which a single word has a link to two or more words but seems logically connected to only one. For example: "The room was not light, but his fingers were." You don't see words like *zeugma* much anymore.

As Rena said, "Therein lies the problem with most of the esoteric vocabulary words. If they are truly obscure, then it's wise not to use them in most newspaper stories unless they are essential to the meaning of the sentence and can be defined for the reader.

"If they are truly obscure and funny, better send them to Charles Osgood. Or work up an act of your own."

Good thoughts. We work with words, but we should use most of the fancy ones just for play or some special use. I like the *News* list, and I like those old lists of beautiful words. But I always wonder why the latter never include my favorites. What do people have against *gangrene* and *incontinence*?

## Metaphors: A Breath of Fresh Air

You can use metaphors and similes to enliven your copy without turning it into gaudy writing.

Try them sometime.

Actually, you already use metaphors regularly. All of us do. Without them, our writing would be considerably barer. We use a metaphor when we refer to a river of protest or a wave of support. When we call a big basketball player a bull, with all the ferocity and power that indicates, we use a metaphor. You know fuller metaphors, too: In "Sail on, o ship of state," the country becomes a vessel. The things that happen to ships can happen metaphorically to countries. For instance, they might founder on rocks of indifference or might be boarded by the twin pirates of inflation and protectionism. Enjoy football? A sportswriter might use a railroad metaphor: *An attempt to flag down the Stanton express train left Midland High flattened on the tracks Friday night.* In that, we have *express train* as a metaphor for the team.

Metaphors differ from similes primarily in that similes liken one thing to another whereas metaphors substitute one for another. That is, a simile normally uses the word *like,* as in "He worked like a beaver," or the word *as,* as in "He's as ugly as week-old guacamole."

You must adhere to four principles in using metaphors and similes: 1. Be appropriate. 2. Be original. 3. Be understandable. 4. Don't go overboard.

Let's run through those principles.

1. An inappropriate metaphor or simile will cause a reader to stumble and to notice the writing. Good writers want to give readers new information quickly and perhaps permanently. They have less interest in getting readers to marvel at the quality of the writing.

So it would be inappropriate, probably, to use a flower in a metaphor for a gang war. That would mean having young men chopped down just as they began to unfold their petals and absorb the sunshine.

You might have, for example, a figure of speech in which you say someone's room is as neat as a monk's moustache. Again, appropriateness depends on circumstances. You might want to say, instead, that it was as neat as a schoolteacher's handwriting. Depends.

Look at that a little further. Say you want to indicate something is as rigid as . . . whatever. You could say it is as rigid or as stiff as a pump handle, but most of today's readers would not have a mental picture of such an object. You might say it is as rigid as a jack handle and get the point across to most. But in some cases a reference to something as rigid as a frozen codfish could be more appropriate. The jack handle would be hard and unyielding, ever unchangeable. The codfish would be temporarily stiff, something that had been changed and could be changed again.

We have other kinds of rigidity. If you refer to self-imposed rigidity, you could mention being as rigid as a Marine drill sergeant's backbone. That would differ a little from something as rigid as the mother superior in a convent; mother superiors, I am told, can be strict, strict disciplinarians, but they have more humanity than drill sergeants. The good writer sees the difference and chooses accordingly.

We also have irony, and in this you refer to someone with all the rigidity of a jellyfish. That works as long as you compose the sentence carefully to cut down on chances of being misunderstood. Many writers have been fooled by overestimating the reader's ability to see through jokes. Ask Art Buchwald about the column in which he said J. Edgar Hoover was not a real person but a made-up name used to fool criminals and others who did not support the FBI. Thousands believed him.

Finally, you can refer to someone as rigid as a jail keeper with a hangover. That gives us a temporary condition, someone who reacts to some external cause. (In this case, the cause can be said to be internal.) You would not use this sort of simile in a deeply serious story.

2. Originality helps. You don't want to reach for cliches, such as the one above in which I refer to a beaver's industriousness. Find something new. Don't refer to coffee that tastes like mud or axle grease; make it taste like heartworm medicine or something scraped off a cowboy's boots or something that dripped out of a veterinarian's black bag.

I sometimes have people create similes by completing this sentence: *Carefully, the two used their shovels to uncover the leaking valve, looking like.* . . . Among the recent answers: "archeologists picking their way into King Tut's tomb," "heart surgeons," "pirates going after buried treasure." These original efforts would all work in some contexts. That is, to repeat, they would be great if appropriate, and not all would be appropriate interchangeably with the others.

3. Metaphors or similes that one cannot understand do more to hurt a story than to help. First, most metaphors and similes need to be used in a short reference. Second, they need to be clear. You must use these bits of wordplay to let readers see things more clearly, or perhaps to let them see things in a new light. One person trying for a metaphor about the Christmas rush said merchants were barricading themselves behind their cash registers to prepare for the attack of the shopping hordes. Interesting. But merchants welcome those hordes, and the reference to a defense indicates otherwise. You can refer to the swarm of shoppers, but you should not confuse your readers with an erroneous reference to unhappy merchants. Sales clerks, maybe.

The principle of being understandable is probably just another plea for appropriateness.

How about a metaphor for the arrival of winter? One workshop participant said winter slipped in under cover of darkness, painted the town white and settled in for a long stay. Another said an unwelcome but regular guest moved into temporary quarters and immediately redecorated everything in an icy lace. Another went military and called winter a fierce invader.

4. Don't go overboard (a metaphor in itself). We had our express train flatten someone on the tracks, and that's enough. We would err if we said this mighty locomotive has quarterback Len Williams at the throttle as it builds up steam and hurtles toward the state championship. Runaway metaphors quickly turn silly.

Let's close with a look at a mixed metaphor or two: *The coach has his head in the sand as his team goes over the precipice. Or, The paper-thin margin will not keep him afloat in the Democratic cauldron.* (Not only hacks and hurried newswriters have this problem. Shakespeare had Hamlet taking arms against a sea of troubles, and you can picture that in your mind.) One more, a triple-header from the real world: *Moose Jaw councilors took the first step toward solving a problem Thursday and threw the city's hat into the ring as the group to spearhead the fight for a new sewer system.*

You see some of that regularly. Get it out of your prose. Work on your writing like a fastidious gardener yanking weeds out of the carrot patch. If you do, I will back you to the hilt when the chips are down.

# The Weakest Verb
## It Is *Is,* Isn't It?

You didn't notice, of course – nor would I had I not been so close to the subject – but the first section of this chapter had a unique quality.

Or at least rare.

Its thousand or so words did not include any form of the infinitive *to be.* No *is.* No *was.* No *will be.* (We had some as auxiliary verbs, but I can't help that.)

I realize this revelation will not likely start a public clamor to have me canonized or drafted by the NBA. Nevertheless, the difficulty of the feat makes it worth discussing.

Let's start with the unprovable assertion above, that this had unique qualities, that no one else wrote such a story. How do I know that? I don't; I just made it up. However, this disease from the Land of Iz taints us all so thoroughly, it stains us so deeply, that I will bet no other word pushers did a story without the word.

Fine. An *is* does the job properly on occasion. Any attempt to ban it will lead to some contrived writing. Inflexible rules can kill you.

But the danger of a rule does not excuse the excesses of our verb. We have no weaker verb than *is.* It says only that something exists. Any professional writer can find something stronger than that. Your vocabulary surely contains a livelier verb that tells us something occurs, that something acts, that something happens. *Is* can't do it; the word has no stamina.

Look around you. Check the copy you wrote yesterday. Full of izzes? Look at out-of-town newspapers. Full of izzes? Read a breakfast cereal label. Or a diet ad. Izzes assault us from every side. They inundate us.

Seeking numbers to support this thesis, I checked the reading room. The first newspaper I picked up had no *is* as the main verb in any of its Page One leads. A disappointment. I was caught in a lie. The next paper used *is* in only three of 10 leads. Hardly an inundation. Then, with relief, I found a paper with six cases of *is* in seven stories – six main predicates. On a previous check of this kind, I had found a story with no other predicate in the first five sentences.

That kind of limp writing won't do.

If we look at this verb carefully, we can see how weak it is. Oops. I mean we can see its weakness. We can see that it does not advance our story, most of the time. Look at some examples, with and without *is*.

> There is nothing that can be done about it. (Nothing can be done about it.)
>
> Farmers in this area are poor. (Farmers in this area don't have enough money to buy this year's seed.)
>
> There are many garages that do not have this service. (Many garages lack this service.)

You try it. Revise the next three sentences: 1. *Is* is a weak verb. 2. *Is* was the main verb in three of 10 leads in one newspaper. 3. This *is* the only story that had no form of the infinitive *to be* in it.

I won't tell you how to fix those; your decision depends on what you need to say. You can say "*Is* lacks power" or "*Is* doesn't advance the story" or "*Is* just lies there," depending on the direction your thoughts run. The others offer similar opportunities for improvement.

You will not have any trouble finding more examples, more challenges. Look for them. Root them out. You will produce stronger action and, usually, a tighter, easier-to-understand sentence.

The main point again: We aren't outlawing the word. Sometimes, *is* is precisely the right word for a situation. At other times— most other times—it weakens your sentence. If that happens, cut it out.

Is that clear?

# Get Rid of It

> More boat ramps and a riverside bicycle-hiking trail will be two priority items in the city's waterfront development plan.

Instead of the weak verb *be,* say the ramps and trail will get priority or emphasis.

> The factor that could be the difference in Saturday's contest is whether or not Mercedes wins its Class 4A play-off game tonight.

Get a little more strength in your verb: *How Mercedes does in its Class 4A play-off game tonight could have a decisive influence on Saturday's contest.*

There was no action by the chamber on the proposal.

Go to active voice with a stronger verb: *The chamber did not act on the proposal.*

There were several factors contributing to the losses.

We combine the weak verb *were* with vagueness (*several*), giving us a sad sentence. Revise once: *Several factors contributed to the losses.* Then revise again to replace *several* with a number. Count the factors.

There is very little that happens on a football field that can escape the comprehension of Jacksonville head coach Ray Durham.

Weak opening. Say: *Little that happens on a football field escapes the comprehension. . . .* Note that we got rid of *very,* one of those enhancers that clutter too much writing.

There was an estimated $8,000 damage done to the car, according to the report.

Get rid of *There is* and *There was.* They just sap your energy. Say: *The car suffered damage estimated at $8,000.* Or: *The car suffered about $8,000 worth of damage, the report said.*

There were exhausted, sweaty bodies strewn all over the field, blood dripping from cut knees and bruises beginning to bloom.

Say: *Exhausted, sweaty bodies adorned the field . . .* or *decorated the field* or *lay strewn about the field.*

He said there are a number of factors that make Marin County different.

Simple. Say this: *He said a number of factors make Marin County different.*

# *Which* and *That*

Somewhere in this country walks a man or woman who with one word struck a blow, possibly unknowingly, against clear writing. This person once said writers should avoid the word *that*. His or her disciples then spread across the land, ridding the nation of a locustlike plague of unnecessary *thats*. Their indiscriminate slaughter of the locusts killed off a lot of honeybees. Too bad. We needed to get rid of superfluous *thats*, but we didn't need to run the word out of the vocabulary. We often use it to pollinate our prose.

Let's look at some sentences with *that* problems:

1. He believes that he knows best.
2. He says that he knows best.
3. He thinks that he knows best.
4. He knows that he can win.
5. She felt her arm, which had thrown 87 pitches, was weak.
6. The company declared a dividend on the stock would not be available this year.
7. She stated her reasons for the policy were sound.
8. He proclaimed his love for the maiden was undying.

You recognize the problem. We must take *that* out of Nos. 1-4 and use it with 5-8. It is not really *wrong* in 1-4; we just don't need it. In 5-8, it throws the reader off a little. You have a transitive verb, *felt*, in No. 5, and one would normally assume an object would follow. With a transitive verb, a subject does something to an object. We thought the subject, *she*, did something (*felt*) to an object (*her arm*). Not so. She felt a clause. The clause says her arm was weak. *Her arm* is the subject in an object clause, not just an object by itself.

You see the same problem in No. 6. The company did not declare a dividend. It declared *that* a dividend would be withheld.

We do not have this problem with 1-4, because the word *he*, as the subject of the object clause, cannot be an object itself. When we see *he*, we know it is the subject of a clause. We do not get misled temporarily.

Some verbs also offer us protection against error with this word. Unlike *felt* (meaning either "fondled" or "believed"), they can be used only one way.

I hate to steal from H.W. Fowler so regularly, but he was kind enough to compile three lists of verbs affected by old *that*. I offer his list, and some other words gathered on my own, for you to think about. If you care about this business of writing, you will make a sentence with each word, at least in your mind.

| *Usually use* that | | *Usually omit* that | *Varies* |
|---|---|---|---|
| agree | indicate | believe | tell |
| announce | learn | presume | confess |
| argue | maintain | suppose | declare |
| assume | note | think | hear |
| calculate | observe | | perceive |
| charge | remark | | promise |
| conceive | state | | say |
| contend | suggest | | see |

Do not consider the list inclusive. The tricky ones in the right column call for care. Run your sentence through your mind both ways, with and without *that*. If it sounds all right without the word, leave it out. If the sentence sounds awkward without *that,* put it in. If you are unsure, use it.

Let's look at one other thought on this word. If you have a sentence in which the first subordinate clause can do without a *that* but the other cannot, use a *that* in both to make them equal. An example:

> The president said he would be there at noon *and that* his intention would be revealed then.

Give this sentence a *that* after *said.* You will make things a little easier on readers. He said that . . . and that. . . . Sometimes, however, you can just as easily balance things by deleting *that* from the second subordinate clause as well as the first. For example, you can delete our word from both of these sentences:

> Jones said they believe the president will see the banners and that he will speak to the bystanders.
> Jones said he thinks he will see the president early in the day and that the deal will quickly go through.

You lose nothing if you delete *that* in both of those. Indeed, you can delete that misused word half the time or more. But you should do so with some thought about rhythm, pace, euphony and all that.

Let me close this part with a thought or two on restrictive clauses and nonrestrictive clauses and their effect on *which* and *that.*

You use *that* with restrictive clauses and *which* with nonrestrictive. That's clear enough. But we need to distinguish between the two kinds of clause, don't we? OK. The restrictive clause limits you to one item or a number of items specified. The nonrestrictive clause merely adds some parenthetical information about the subject.

So we have something like this with a restrictive clause:

Use the first car that has a full tank.

That tells you that you may have to check three or four cars. You mustn't take just any one. Take the first one that has gas.

Nonrestrictive clauses go like this:

Take the blue car, which is over by the gate.

We tell you which one to take, the blue one, and then we throw in some parenthetical remark about where it is. Before we would need a restrictive clause with our blue car we would have to have more than one blue car. We could tell people to take the blue car that is by the gate, as opposed to the blue car behind the shed.

Our material goes the other way on the gassed-up car, too. We can tell someone to take the first car, which has a full tank. That means we direct a person to a car and then throw in, parenthetically, information about the state of the vehicle's fuel.

If you need a simpler way, note that you have commas when you use *which* and you do not have commas with *that.* Easy. Sort of.

# Sexist Pronouns: He/She Said to Him or Her

Julie Bird, meet Tom Berner.

Bird did a newspaper column citing sexism in a lot of places, including, at times, the news columns.

Berner, a professor of journalism at Penn State, once did a commentary on feminist editors; it ran in *Quill,* the magazine of the Society of Professional Journalists.

Bird was justifiably concerned about sexism.

So was Berner.

But I don't think the two of them would be angry at each other. They might even come up with a synthesis: Let's get rid of sexism in the newsroom and news columns, but let's not work at it so hard that we hinder communication.

Some of Bird's complaints have been addressed by the AP-UPI stylebook committee and by journalism organizations. You will find a consensus that we need to replace many of the *-man* terms—*fireman, newsman, policeman, mailman*—with neutrals: *firefighter, reporter/editor/journalist, the police, mail carriers.*

I used to talk about the slot man; he's now the copy chief, partly because he may be a she and I don't want to be inaccurate. There's more: If we always refer to these jobs with masculine titles, do we not discourage women's aspirations for them? I think we do; Bird is positive of it.

On the other hand, *chairman* doesn't bother me in the least. Nor does it bother a woman department head where I work; she calls herself the chairman. I don't object to *director,* but we commit an inaccuracy when we use it, most of the time. If you want to refer to a female committee head as a chairwoman, I would tell you to go ahead. You need to be consistent, though.

We have another area to work on: pronouns. In English, we have traditionally used *he* as the pronoun for singular nouns: *If anyone wants to go, he should pack now.* I object to the use of *he/she should pack* as unnatural. Less forced but still cumbersome is *he or she should pack.* That would be my reluctant second choice. First would be to strive for a plural noun: *People who want to go should pack now.* Then I would stick with the singular *he,* despite flak. Then would come *he or she.* But I would opt for a plain *he* if the time seemed ripe and I thought I wouldn't get an arrow in the chest. The easiest solution, again, is to get a plural noun.

Bird also mentioned the move toward identifying women by last name only, on the second reference. She likes it. It makes sense. I do not know how I would feel if we had a male equivalent of *Miss,* something that would tell us whether a man was married. No need for it, though. My marital status doesn't have anything to do with most of my work, nor Bird's hers, nor Berner's his.

Oh, Bird is young and has youth's tendency to want a fresh start on all traditions. She doesn't realize that many women who get their names in the paper have a connection to a man that might be a legitimate part of an identification. (Example: politicians' wives.) The Associated Press made a start toward eliminating these honorifics, but it found that many women want them. It shied away from *Ms.* for a time, but then it yielded to women who want that title.

No matter what you do, the world's worst excuse is, "But we've always done it that way."

Berner's problem was with a feminist editor on a book he was doing. She changed members of the Printing Pressman's Union No. 2 from *pressmen* to *press people*. And she changed a reference to a child being taken away from its mother to one being taken away from its *mother or other caretaker.*

People like that undercut the work that people like Bird are trying to do. We should get rid of sexist references, out of fairness. But some of us will bow our necks and reach new heights of stubbornness if we get the Berner treatment. The editor committed a foul deed. Anyone with sensitivity would be expected to scream if such a thing was done to him.

Or her.

# Dangling Dangers: When Reading, These Can Fool You

Searching for a column topic, an idea burst upon me: I should do something on dangling modifiers. Care was required, of course; being sophisticated, a grammar trick would never get by readers of a book like this.

Careful with their language, a deviation would immediately be spotted by word watchers. Thinking of ways to offset this, a scheme took shape, calling for use of examples from daily reading.

Usually less contrived than the sentences above, I find a lot of dangling participles in newspapers. Produced unwittingly, you will find many examples of almost ludicrous phrasing in newspapers. Written in total seriousness, many reporters do stories that provide great pleasure to word watchers.

Unable to sustain this thin joke any longer, will you let me switch to a straighter approach? You surely recognize dangling modifiers by now.

Dangling modifiers indicate carelessness more than ignorance. Writers put all the elements into a sentence, but in their haste they neglect to get things lined up. They come close, but they wind up modifying the wrong part of the sentence.

You can avoid the problem by making sure the material right before the comma refers to the material right after it. Let's look at some danglers from newspapers:

Once cooked, they topped the bread with assorted seasonings.

That does not miss by far; readers can puzzle it out. But readers are not supposed to have to puzzle things out. They are not supposed to be misled. They are not supposed to think we are cooking people instead of bread. Writing calls for precision, and that means care. In case you don't see it, for material on either side of the comma we have: *Once cooked, they.* . . . Revise it.

While driving along Highway 111, the community seems more like a resort hotel.

The problem: *While driving, the community.* . . . We have to keep those communities off the highway. Make it: *As you drive along Highway 111.* . . . Or: *From Highway 111.* . . .

Walking through the front door, a variety of Jamaica Joe's labels, an old bench, and a counter hardly signal a business that has distributed more than 21 million shirts around the United States.

We know this meant: *As the visitor walks through the front door.* . . . But that's not what it said.

Being a nonsmoker, my lungs had to adjust.

Who's the nonsmoker, you or your lungs? You. So: *Being a nonsmoker, I needed time for my lungs to adjust.*

While dining at a friend's house over the holidays, my hostess insisted I sample the dessert she had lovingly prepared.

Possible but unlikely. The hostess did not dine at a friend's house; the writer did. Again, precision.

The most highly recruited basketball player in the history of Orange County, Lewis' services are coveted by all the biggies.

You cannot make *services* into a player. We get this error regularly, but not from careful writers.

After owning the vehicle four months, Bibby said, the transmission began to leak.

The attribution, though proper, probably threw the writer off. The writer saw a good subject, or thought he did, in *Bibby*. But *transmission* had a better claim to being the subject; so it appropriated the modifier. If you delete the attribution, which is parenthetical and thus subject to deletion, you have this start: *After owning the vehicle for four months, the transmission began to leak.* Do this: *After owning the vehicle for four months, Bibby said, he noticed the transmission had begun to leak.*

> Once removed to the Cobb home, the Mullins employees reassembled the tank.

This says: *Once removed . . . , the employees. . . .* That could have happened, but it didn't in this case. Only the tank got moved to the Cobb home. The writer erred.

> Rushing in the door after a busy day at school, a youngster's first thought is often an after-school snack.

Fools rush in, but thoughts don't. We have to say: *Rushing in the door after a busy day at school, a youngster often thinks first of a snack.*

> Like any other bird farmer, the noise is music to his ears.

Not quite. Say: *Like any other bird farmer, he thinks the noise has the sound of music.*

> The ship is a bit dusty from its trip to the city, but after a good bath and some minor repairs, Gruber plans to exhibit the craft.

Instead of preparing Mr. Gruber a warm tub, we need to sharpen our writing. I have departed from dangling participles for this final example, but the problem remains: Those modifying clauses cannot be twisted. They modify the subject unless you work out some other approach. To wit: *But after giving it a good bath and some minor repairs, Gruber plans. . . .* Or: *But after it gets a good bath and some minor repairs, Gruber plans to exhibit the craft.*

When dangling, watch those modifiers.

# Cliches: They're as Thick as Hops

Most of us could improve our writing if we got rid of some of our friends.

We have these old friends we call upon any time we need a convenient phrase. They stand around, always ready. And we put them to work every time we write. Some of them grow weary from overwork.

These friends are commonly called cliches, and they appear in writing at almost all levels. News writers and others who work in haste rely on them. Politicians use them to save everyone the effort of thinking. They surround us. They suffocate us.

My interest in cliches was revived by an Eric Partridge book, *A Dictionary of Cliches.* Partridge, who died in 1979, chased cliches for five decades or more. He found enough of them to get this dictionary through five editions. Of course, this chase did not require visits to exotic lands; cliches can be found everywhere. Tracing their origins was the hard part.

I commend the book to you, not because you need a supply of new cliches but because you need to remind yourself just how stale some of your regular pals are. Or at least I did. (Write Broadway House, 9 Park St., Boston, MA 02108.)

A cliche is a stereotyped expression, a worn-out, commonplace phrase that comes readily to mind.

Partridge put it this way: "A cliche is a phrase or short sentence that careful speakers and scrupulous writers shrink from because they feel that its use is an insult to the intelligence of the audience or the public."

Note the word *scrupulous.* That lets too many of us out.

Cliches are bred by laziness and encouraged by haste. Rather than go for a precise term, we turn to the handy cliche. And our writing suffers.

I need to mention that cliches are not limited to oldies (*The bigger they are, the harder they fall*) or to metaphors (*ship of state; nipped in the bud*) or similes (*sank like a rock; a voice like thunder*). We all recognize those trite sayings as cliches. We avoid them. But we don't boggle at dark horses and bitter ends and breaths of fresh air and people who work behind the scenes. We use these terms because they let us fill a page without having to think about what we are communicating.

The trouble is that cliches force us to abandon precision in our work. Not to mention flavor. Or vigor. Or care.

All this has a horrifying side effect, too: Undiscerning readers become so accustomed to cliches that they think cliches are a sign of cleverness. So we get a circle.

I often tell young people to read widely as they learn to write. I must adjust that and tell them to be careful to pick up only the good habits of writers. Gather the jewels; leave the trash.

Some people have even argued that broadcast audiences expect, possibly demand, cliches. We expect to be told regularly that Tom Landry is the only coach the Dallas Cowboys have ever had, or that a team faces a punting situation. Or that Mark Gastineau gives 110 percent. Or that Danny White is still struggling to get out of Roger Staubach's shadow. Our expectation indicates only our own degeneracy; broadcasters who pander to it are degenerates of another class.

Broadcasters did not invent all our cliches. Most cliches start life as idioms, nice little phrases that convey special meaning, apart from the literal. Try *bolt from the blue*. Or *steady as a rock*. Or *six of one and half a dozen of the other*. All these had meanings, nearly literal, that became blunted by indiscriminate overexposure.

They served us well. They were good friends. But now they have turned and become enemies of good writing.

Tell them good-bye.

# Contractions: Don't Be Afraid of Them

People who write about the language run the risk of having a mild expression of disapproval translated into a flat prohibition. So let's agree right up front that we like contractions. I like them. I use them. I encourage you to use them.

With some thought.

Contractions take some of the sting of formality out of writing, even the semiformal writing that newspapers require. If not overdone, they help readers understand a story better—they are nearer the reader's customary speech than are the longer versions. (Timid writers have trouble with this advice, because they worry about the word *overdone*. They spend too much time in the shallow end of the pool, and they could be enjoying a swim. Dive in; just don't stay in so long you drown.)

You can't, or cannot, imagine Humphrey Bogart saying this: "Here is looking at you, kid." It's unnatural. How about Superman's fans: "It is a bird. It is a plane. It is Superman!"

No. *It's* gets more calls than *It is,* and it should.

But not all contractions deserve our blessing. I object to two kinds: 1. The interloper, or pseudocontraction. Call it the illegitimate cousin. 2. The regular contraction that gets put to an irregular use.

You know the interlopers. Take *he'd,* for example. Or, worse, *they'dve.* Please take them, far away. Those aren't real words. At best, *he'd* deserves to be shot for ambiguity. It doesn't even have a normal written use. We use it in spoken language, where we have control over inflection and where we get even more informal than in writing. It probably means *he had.* The saving is not worth the effort it costs readers.

As for *they'dve,* forget that one. The proper spelling probably goes like this: *they'd of.* We're just spelling out our mispronunciation of *they would have.* We do this on others, too, unfortunately. This is what I mean when I say newspapers should be just a little above the informal language of speech. Not much. A little.

Then we have the irregular uses I mentioned. Here's one from a newspaper:

> The developer of the proposed $9 million Harbor Town Marina said Thursday he's received final federal approval for the project.

We err in using *he's,* because readers are more likely to think of it as *he is* than as *he has,* the meaning we want. The ambiguity slows readers down. Good writers do not put up impediments to speedy reading. We have the same trouble with *he'd. He'd* can mean *he had* or *he would.* Readers will have to do more work than they like. For example:

> Jones said he'd done his best.
> Jones said he'd be here early Monday.

I don't mean a literate reader cannot glean the proper meaning, but the words do slow us.

Let's see what we can do about some guidelines for acceptable contractions.

1. Generally, you can comfortably use contractions involving *not.* That covers a large number of words such as *isn't, can't, won't* and *aren't.* It does not include *ain't,* but you know that.

2. You should avoid contractions of verbs standing alone at the end of a sentence. You see the flaw in this: *The Tigers wonder who else is going to the state meet. They know for sure they're.* I had to force that

one, but you see the problem. If not, get help. If no one else will help,
I'll.

3. Let your ear guide you with the helping verbs, the auxilia-
ries. In this country, you can get away with *They've done their best,* but
you miss with *They've no reason to try that.* The British would accept
the second sentence. They've been doing it for centuries.

4. You can usually contract the word *is,* a slovenly verb in the
first place. You can say things like these: *Here's a new idea. There's a
time for everything.* (Look at the early part of this chapter for further
criticism of this verb.)

5. If you have any doubts about ambiguity, don't use the contraction. For example:

> Just one month into a probe of available social services, the League of
> Women Voters has learned the county's short on services and long on
> problems.

Deep in a sentence that way, *county's* looks like a possessive.
You will mislead readers for a moment or more. Try one more:

> The government bailed out Chrysler when it was sinking and it's
> pumped money into foreign nations when they were in need.

Some will see *it's* as *it is* and some as *it has.* We are more
accustomed to *it is,* which happens to be wrong here. Actually, this
sentence has double ambiguity, for the word *it* refers to Chrysler first
and then to the government.

So there you have some simple advice. Use the standard contractions but stay away from the oddballs. If in doubt, skip the contraction. You'll be OK.

# 4

# So Many Ways to Err

Writing sins ● *Vagueness. Wordiness. Quotation and attribution misuse.*
*Weak starts. Passivity. Punctuation carelessness. The* willbe *syndrome. Pronoun*
*bewilderment. Misplaced time elements.* Which/that *woes. Sputtering speech*
*stories. Potpourri.* More sins ● Punctuation ● *Commas. Some*
*punctuating practice.* Misplaced modifiers ● Downtrodden
irregular verbs ● Don't be so negative

## Writing Sins

I prefer the positive approach to the negative, but a lot of any
discussion of writing will necessarily involve some prohibitions: Don't
do this; don't do that. We're going to take a look at recurring writing
flaws, and that involves negatives — bad things, the problems I note
most often in reading newspapers. We can hit some broad problems
first and then trickle down into common spelling errors and other little
items.

Some of these deserve — and get — fuller treatment elsewhere
in this volume. I'm just offering a sampling for the moment.

### Vagueness

Start with the word *several,* almost always a sign of laziness,
ignorance or inexperience. A report of a speech noted that "several
other speakers" addressed the audience. You don't have to be a genius
to count; in this case it was four, as the story eventually showed. Let
me give you a better example: *Looking toward the future, Brightsville*

*Memorial District directors yesterday took several actions to shore up the district's defenses against losing revenue this year.*

How many actions? We don't know. But we should be told. You should simply count and list the actions, probably in order of importance, and then go down your list and discuss each one. Not only would you eliminate vagueness, but you would also make your story easier to read and to write.

If the city editor will send a reporter back to get the number instead of loafing through with *several,* the world will be a nicer place.

## Wordiness

I have seen leads as long as 90 words, and 45-worders are plentiful. See this: ....... That's a string of periods. When you run into a 45-word lead, find a place to put one of those periods. A little revision into two 25-worders would make things much easier to understand — most of the time. You can still be literate. Just be more considerate of readers and use relatively few 30-word sentences.

## Quotation and Attribution Misuse

My major complaint about quotations is that we sometimes forget them. Quotations make stories more human. Almost all stories need them. You write a paragraph of summary and then hit the reader with a little quotation that makes your summary clearer. Don't make quotations do all the expository work. Another thought: I hesitate to make broad generalizations about excessive attribution, but we do have too much. We do not need to attribute most statements of easily ascertainable fact. If our story mentions that a person who got a grant was in charge of four others, that doesn't require attribution. Ditto if we say he got his grant from the state. Or he used seeds from the state college. No danger there. But if we say his new tomatoes are likely to wipe out world hunger, we have a statement we cannot stand behind, a fact not easily ascertainable, and we must attribute it to someone or qualify it some other way.

## Weak Starts

*There is/there are.* You cannot find a weaker beginning for a sentence. *There is* merely tells us that something exists. You can improve nearly every sentence it begins. Avoid it.

## Passivity

You can strengthen most passive-voice sentences with a switch to active. Witness: *The pillars were pulled down by Samson,* as opposed to *Samson pulled down the pillars.* Nearly all leads are better in the active voice. Tell us that an airplane struck the tower, not that the tower was struck by a plane.

## Punctuation Carelessness

We have an abundance of problems with one little punctuation mark, the comma. I give you 12 rules governing commas in the section called "Punctuation" in this chapter. I won't go over them here, but I will say that we continue to err with great regularity. Every newsroom ought to have a handbook of English usage.

## The *Willbe* Syndrome

Example: *The Longhorns will be facing the Shorthorns.* Why not just *will face?*

## Pronoun Bewilderment

The advertising people have done us in. They say: *Everyone should try their hardest. Every student can get their grades tomorrow.* If you don't want to use *his,* the singular pronoun, say *his or her.* Or say *students* (plural) can get *their grades* (also plural). You had a fuller dose of this in a section called "Sexist Pronouns," in Chapter 3.

## Misplaced Time Elements

We get this: *Air traffic controllers today did not return to work and President Reagan said they were fired.* The time element normally works best behind the verb: *. . . did not return to work today. . . .* Try it there; sometimes it has to go elsewhere. But not often. (See "Time Element" in Chapter 5.)

## Which/That Woes

We struggle with these more than anything else. Rule of thumb: *Which* normally takes commas. It goes on nonrestrictive clauses. *That* goes on restrictive clauses. *Wait for the seventh car that has its lights on.* That sentence means we may wait for a hundred cars. The seventh with lights is the one we want; we restrict ourselves to No. 7. Contrast that with: *Wait for the seventh car, which has its lights on.* Now we wait for the seventh car. We use the nonrestrictive clause to add some information about that car. We set that clause off with a comma.

## Sputtering Speech Stories

I am constantly amazed – no, dismayed – by writers who start a speech story by saying someone spoke. Students get an F in my class if they begin a speech story that way. Such a lead could have been written a month earlier. Basic rule: If the speaker doesn't say something worth reporting, we shouldn't run a story in the first place. Look for the news.

## Potpourri

Then we have *strangled to death.* Just *strangled* will do. And how about *compare to?* You use *compare to* for likening unlike things; you use *compare with* for looking at similarities and differences of like things. You compare a helicopter to a hummingbird. You compare a Ford with a Chevrolet.

Next we have *due to. Due to* is adjectival. It modifies a noun, as in: *His wealth was due to his cleverness.* So we err in saying: *He quit the team due to a falling-out with the coach.* He quit *because of* a falling out. His departure (a noun) was *due to* the falling-out (adjectival).

I also see *alot* for *a lot, alright* for *all right* and *towards* and *afterwards* for words that don't have an *s* on the end. I also see *affect* and *effect* misused; each has a place. I see the word *lay* abused regularly, as in: *Let's go lay on the beach and catch some sun.* You need *lie* there. *Lay* is the past tense of *lie.* You can say: *We lay on the beach this morning.* (When you put something down, *lay* is the present tense. *I will lay your watch on the shelf.* For the past tense, you use *laid,* as in: *I laid your watch on the table just a minute ago.* This verb takes some work, because it holds the record for irregularity. So work on it.

We'll close with a sentence that cheats us out of an *and: These people are conservative, religious, competitive, family-oriented and work hard at their jobs.* They *are* conservative. They *are* religious. They *are* competitive. They *are* family-oriented. And they *are* work hard at their jobs? No. We need another *and*. Our people *are* the first four things; and then they *do* the last one. These people are conservative, religious, competitive, and family-oriented, *and they work hard at their jobs*.

# More Sins

We have been discussing minor sins that plague our business. Lapses in grammar are minor sins. Errors of fact are major sins.

A publisher-friend offered a list of thou-shalt-nots that included the use of *it was reported* to tag a sentence. I can relate to that. We see that phrase often. Here is his example: *The voter turnout was heavy, it was reported*. He has the correct idea on that. On ascertainable facts, we ought not fall back on such terminology. Reporters ought to find out the facts. If they can't, they ought to at least pinpoint their source.

We probably have two reasons for using the phrase: 1. It lets us put in the date and thus appear to be offering something fresh. 2. It takes us off the hook by making a flat statement and then laying it off on someone else.

Even so, we are better off revising sentences that say something like this: *The president has two more alternative plans for freeing the Iranian hostages, it was reported Tuesday*. Tell us who reported it.

I'm not trying to offer you something as a guaranteed way to fix up such phrasing. I just want to remind you to think about changing a sentence with that phrase in it.

The same publisher also objects to meeting stories that say a number of people *were in attendance*. He's right. *Attended* will do every time. Better still, of course, is to slip the information in sideways with clauses like these:

> Speaking to a crowd of 150 at the armory, Elred said. . . .
> The audience of 150 students cheered when Elred. . . .
> Elred told the crowd of 150 young Indians that. . . .

That brings us to *only*.

This little word gets shunted around all over the place. It has precise work to do, but some people throw it in almost willy-nilly. Be careful with it. Remember Strunk and White's special sentence: *I hit him in the eye yesterday*. You can insert an *only* before each word, in turn, and get multiple meanings from that one.

*Only* has a troublesome first cousin, *not only*. The main thing about *not only* is that we have to have our following items parallel. That is, if the word after the *not only* is a verb, the word after *but* or *but also* should be a verb, too. As in: *He not only drinks but dips snuff.* Same with adjectives: *She is not only beautiful but smart.* And nouns: *The academy accepted not only Bill but Pete.*

Imperfection steals in. Sometimes we get such abominations as this: *The academy not only accepted Bill but also Pete.*

Another member of that family is the *either/or* bit. You need parallelism there, too. But we get errors such as this: *He will either fight Archie Moore or Rocky Graziano.* As with *not only,* you need to get the same kinds of parts of speech behind the *either* and the *or. He will either fight* (verb) *Archie Moore or meet* (verb) *Rocky Graziano. He will meet either Archie Moore* (noun) *or Rocky Graziano* (noun).

Yes. I am aware that we all know this stuff. It's just that we get in a hurry and don't tidy up our own mistakes. My job is to remind you to do the necessary cleanup.

# Punctuation
## Commas

The comma, the lowly, simple comma, gives writers more trouble than any other punctuation mark. We see it misused and abused in all kinds of newspapers.

Sometimes a writer misses the comma key or taps it too lightly. Sometimes writers let their tired fingers sag onto sensitive VDT keys, giving us extra commas; all kinds of mechanical things can happen.

Most of our problems have other origins. They grow from inattention or from lack of knowledge. Young writers like to eliminate a comma if it would fall about where a TV announcer would grab a breath. If asked to read their work aloud, they pause naturally at the proper place, though they feel no need to write a comma there. If they know to pause, they reason, a reader would know to pause; therefore, the comma is unneeded.

Nonsense.

Readers are not supposed to have to guess what the writer had in mind. Proper punctuation helps tell readers exactly what is meant, exactly where a pause belongs. It gives readers precise directions, rather than letting them take a guess.

Take this sentence: *Let's eat Grandma.* Some writers have no problem with that, assuming a reader will supply the pause. They think readers will instantly recognize this as a form of direct address to Grandma.

Such writers call for extra work by readers. You force readers to drag themselves back on track after being pushed off. If they believe the punctuation, they think the quotation comes from a group of cannibals discussing the menu for a family picnic. A precise writer cannot run the risk of being misunderstood that way.

Let's look at some of the rules governing commas. You can add to or alter the list, no doubt. Don't think I am showing off; I have to look these up in my handbook. (A number of publishers put out good handbooks, some almost as good as my old Harbrace from college. I steal from them all.)

Anyway, we use commas to do these things:

1. Separate words in a series of three or more, except before the last item. English teachers thresh about in anguish over that last point. They want two commas in *hostile, agile and mobile*. (The AP-UPI stylebook illustrates the point with *red, white and blue*.) We journalists are right, as usual, because the comma replaces the *and* in a series, and you normally do not need the comma if you have an *and*. You would not say something was "red, and white." I'll get back to this point in a minute.

2. Set off nonrestrictive clauses. Such clauses add to the meaning of whatever they refer to. They do not restrict it. Example: *The work, which I enjoy, pays handsomely.* The restrictive version would say: *The work that I enjoy pays handsomely.*

3. Set off nonrestrictive appositives. An appositive is a noun that renames another noun. *John Jones, the manager, paid the bar tab for all.*

4. Set off a subordinate clause preceding the main clause. This refers to clauses that start with words like *because, if* and *unless*. Like this: *If he is right, we are in serious trouble.*

5. Separate equal adjectives in a series: *We are in deep, everlasting trouble. Deep* and *everlasting* are equals. The comma does not separate unequal adjectives, those that modify the string. As in this: *We look forward to an exciting weekend football game.* That does not refer to an exciting game, a weekend game and a football game, just an exciting weekend football game. The stylebook says it more clearly, perhaps, referring to the old oaken bucket and a cheap fur coat. *Fur coat* and *oaken bucket* are noun phrases, just as *football game* is a noun phrase, exciting or not.

6. Set off words used in direct address, as in: *Smile when you*

*say that, stranger.* Or, *Come here, Mr. Watson.* We do not use much direct address in news columns.

7. Set off equal clauses joined by a conjunction: *This material is hard to handle, but we need to understand it.* In that one, we set off compound sentences but not compound verbs. Compound verbs? Delete the comma in sentences like this: *He likes it, but won't pay for it.*

8. Set off words that slightly interrupt a sentence: *Reporters, unlike editors, must go out into the weather.*

9. Set off short quotations: *He said, "I think that's enough for now."* We use colons to set off multisentence quotes.

10. Set off an attribution after a statement: *The moon will be full tonight, Jones said.* You do not use the comma the other way around (*Jones said the moon will be full tonight*), except for a quotation: *Jones said, "The moon will be full tonight."*

11. Set off parenthetical expressions: *Ronald Reagan, once a movie star, has done well for himself lately.*

12. Set off a beginning participle phrase from a main clause: *Staring at his four mashed toes, he completely forgot about his toothache.*

Some other thoughts. Commas are not strong enough to handle an abrupt interruption. You need dashes or parentheses for that: *The best writers—those who work at their craft—will always do well.* You get slightly less emphasis with parentheses: *The best writers (as judged in this survey) will always do well.*

We also have the comma splice problem to put to rest. You see it when someone tries to join two coordinate clauses without a conjunction: *She needs to get out of the sun, her makeup will run.* Use a period or at least a semicolon.

We close with one other thought. Do not follow any rule out the window. Violate a rule if the violation contributes to better understanding. Scrap a rule before you scrap common sense. Here's a made-up example of zealotry with rules: *The staff includes a former beauty queen, a woman who can type, a baseball player, the inventor of the pica pole, a middle-aged man with an obsession for shooting skeet and young girls—all of whom are hard workers.*

Under Rule 1, we do not need a comma before *and young girls.* Common sense tells us we do. Otherwise, readers will think our skeet shooter takes illegal target practice. That would be as bad as having an unnecessary, comma in our copy.

Many of the preceding thoughts appeared in *Publisher's Auxiliary.* Much of the follow-up in the next section appeared in newspapers. You get a quiz now. Decide which rule is violated. The answers are at the end.

1. The United States is at war with terrorists and how newsmen cover their activities could help or impede the effort.
2. It is 8,000 feet high at the base where the tram begins its ascent to the top where panoramic views are breathtaking.
3. The Eagles . . . just wore down a smaller, but game Buckeye Central defense.
4. Holden and Molinar have known each other since 1964, when they began salvage operations with famed salvor, Mel Fisher.
5. Sorry Oilers, Bud's part of the deal
6. Look out 'Crocodile Dundee'
7. Before buying the Florida ranch listen to your wife's concerns.
8. Worst coming says former meteorologist
9. Nebraska increasing pace in efforts to attract industry says DED director
10. Schools: Be there students

Answers: (1) Rule 7. (2) 2; put commas after *base, ascent* and *top.* (3) 7; kill the comma. (4) 3, sort of; see below. (5) 6. (6) 6. (7) 12. (8) 10. (9) 10. (10) 6.

About that No. 4. You can use a comma if you refer to *A famed salvor, Mel Fisher.* But if you use the words as a title, you need no comma. You can refer to *UT quarterback Brett Stafford.* You can refer to *the UT quarterback, Brett Stafford.* You can even talk about *UT's quarterback, Brett Stafford.* But you cannot mix title and appositive; you cannot refer to *UT quarterback, Brett Stafford.* I see this on *city commissioner, Bill Smith.* And *county attorney, Earl Monroe.* Use a comma without titles or throw in a set of commas for something you put in apposition.

# Some Punctuating Practice

They were approved from 1979-85.

The hyphen joins things rather than separates them. If you want to show a span, you must say 1979 to 1985. Or if you want to make it one time period, you say they were approved in 1979-85.

Most students were shaken, but unhurt.

They were shaken but unhurt. No comma. Or you could say: *Most students were shaken, but they were unhurt.* That gives you a comma to separate two independent clauses. Short parallel items need no commas: *short but fast, lean but mean, amiable but deceptive, sweet but changeable.*

> The Kinglyton Toastmasters Club has met for its second meeting in April with President, Palmer Dixon, presiding.

This came from a correspondent, and we are happy to have correspondents bring in material. However, we need to get them to write better or we need to find the time for a rewrite. Let us concentrate only on the punctuation problem, the pair of unnecessary commas. Titles used as titles before a name do not take commas. Call our man President Palmer Dixon. If you want to use a title as an appositive, you must have an article, as in this: *The president, Palmer Dixon, directed the program.* You can say this about someone: *He dated cheerleader Betsy Boop.* Or you can say: *He dated Betsy Boop, a cheerleader.* The latter version gets you away from something some newspapers object to as a false title. Some publications, particularly newsmagazines, go overboard on false titles. For a bad example, try a reference to an athlete as Sidearm Pitching Star Ewell Blackwell.

> A fire touched off an explosion that sent sulfurous, yellow dust into the west Odessa sky Thursday.

That's not wrong. But you can help readers by cutting out a comma if you refer to *sulfurous yellow dust.* Sounds better. We are not trying to refer to the distinctively separate qualities of the dust. We would use a comma in referring to a short, poker-faced man or a tall, long-legged woman, because we cite single qualities.

> They include Renaldo who is blind, Mark who has cerebral palsy, Mandy who is deaf and a little girl who wears glasses named Melody.

No. This says she named her specs. Get *named Melody* after *little girl.* Let's also work on the punctuation. Those clauses in apposition (for example, *who is blind, who has cerebral palsy, who is deaf* and *who wears glasses*) must be set off. Usually we set them off with commas. In this case, we have a series, so we should use commas and semicolons. Yes, you use a semicolon after the next-to-last item in such a series. So: *They include Renaldo, who is blind; Mark, who has cerebral palsy; Mandy, who is deaf; and a little girl named Melody, who wears glasses.*

"It's got to be replaced, we can't leave it the way it is, IBWC is going to make us do something I'm sure," Quilio said.

Even in a quote you can provide proper punctuation. We need two periods here (after *replaced* and *it is*), because those clauses cannot be spliced together with commas. We also need a comma before *I'm sure.*

The Panthers drilled 14-of-16 charity tosses in the fourth quarter.

A century or so ago, shortly after the first sports story was written, some sportswriter put hyphens in a phrase like that. The disease spread. Sportswriters do not want to think; they just throw in the hyphens. A waste. We could use hyphens if we referred to a *14-for-16 performance in free throws,* but *14-for-16* would be an adjective. Let me change the sentence a little, though its grammatical structure remains the same. You will see the logic behind elimination of hyphens: *He hit 14 of his 16 free throws.* Drop *his* and then avoid those hyphens.

# Misplaced Modifiers

An interest in writing tends to feed upon itself. The more you study this business, the more you see ways to improve.

Take the problem we have with getting modifiers next to clauses they modify. For example, in a TV ad, Ed McMahon said he had some information for us. A voice-over pitchman came on and said, "You will soon receive the information in the mail that Mr. McMahon mentioned." Wrong. Mr. McMahon didn't mention any mail; he mentioned only the information. Our pitchman put the modifier next to *mail,* the wrong word.

The error is not confined to TV pitchmen. News writers commonly let some distance creep between the two elements—the modifier and the word modified. The ear is offended, but the offense falls short of criminality and we overlook the error. Only when we get a full case of assault do we sit up and complain.

People with enough interest to complain about that problem get their sensitivity level raised. They start finding other kinds of problems in writing. They give writing a hard look. If they look in their own copy—rather than just criticizing others' work—they can improve their writing.

The improvement takes effort. Simple changes do not always provide the best solution. Sometimes we have to rewrite sentences completely. We get interested in doing that, and we start looking at all parts of our writing more carefully. Hence the observation above that an interest in writing feeds upon itself.

The more you look, the more you run across the problem of misplaced modifiers. You simply have to remember that the modifying clause must go next to the item modified.

Let's look at some examples. Some can be handled with an editing stroke, and some require rewriting.

In the Ed McMahon bit, one little change would take care of things: *You will soon receive in the mail the information Mr. McMahon mentioned.* That gets *information* next to the modifier, the clause that tells which information we have in mind. A simpler approach would be to say that the information he mentioned will soon be mailed to us.

Writers have to decide which path to take.

If you develop an awareness of the problem, probably by going over your own or others' work, you can sometimes head off the problem by mentally rewriting as you go along. With enough awareness, you never write an awkward sentence that has to be recast.

I lie. All writers have to revise.

Let's look at some more examples.

Hundreds of schoolchildren had climbed the mountain with their teachers and rucksacks on their backs.

Strong little rascals, aren't they? We can use a straight change and put the rucksacks next to children: *Hundreds of children with rucksacks on their backs had climbed the mountain with their teachers.* If we wanted to, we could shorten that a bit: *Hundreds of children wearing rucksacks. . . .*

Nearby was the food table, presided over by Betty Parker, filled with delicious cakes.

Although such a situation could occur, I suspect the reader was describing the dining hall rather than Miss Parker's diet. So we have to shake things around a little. (Be careful and don't jostle Miss Parker; that much cake could make her dangerous.) We say: *Nearby was the food table, filled with delicious cakes and presided over by Betty Parker.* If we want to put more emphasis on our hostess, we start with: *Nearby, Betty Parker presided over the food table. . . .* Writers look for options, for ways of saying precisely what they want, with no chance for a mistake by readers.

> The board has passed an ordinance that outlaws cows grazing by the roadside and riding bicycles on the sidewalks.

Well, our city's cattle are more athletic than most, but we can corral them with some reorganization. Try this, with a change of verbs: *The board has made the city's sidewalks off limits to bicycle riders and has decided that cows can no longer legally graze by the roadside.*

> In 1974, Conrad began an association that lasted practically uninterrupted until his death when he became head clerk of the Alamo Hotel.

No, we don't have ghost clerks. We could shift the *when he became* clause around with commas: *In 1974, when he became head clerk of the Alamo Hotel, Conrad began an association that lasted practically uninterrupted until his death.* The sentence does not sing, what with the punctuation and two clauses before the subject and predicate. Still, we have improved it. And that's a start.

The problem even crops up in headlines. Take this one: *Parents ask court to keep dog that bit daughter away.* You must put *away* next to *keep.* But that will sound stilted. This headline would be better off with a total revision, probably just asking the court to restrain the mutt.

> Smith, who will accompany the birds south, said one was found almost frozen because of a cold snap by a woman.

We have to get that woman in front of our cold bird: *Smith, who will accompany the birds south, said a woman found one bird almost frozen after a cold snap.*

> "I'm tired," said Lois Howard, whose 17-year-old son is in jail and who is a grade school teacher in Denver.

With this, we have the problem of ambiguity. Well, actually we have less ambiguity than we have pure error. We have made a teacher of the boy. We have to call the woman *a Denver grade school teacher whose 17-year-old son is in jail.*

That brings us to tricky words, as in this:

> Liquor store owners heard advice about how to protect themselves from Police Chief Ambrose Bierce.

Mr. Bierce does not prey on liquor store operators, so an adjustment is required. We cannot get by with simply rearranging the given words. We have to throw in some new ones: *Police Chief Ambrose Bierce told liquor store owners how they can protect themselves.*

> The cycle was disrupted by hard freezes in January and February that damaged lawns and shrubbery.

There we threw in the time element in what appeared to be a convenient place, but it separated the clause about freezes and damage. So we have to say: *The cycle was disrupted in January and February by hard freezes that damaged lawns and shrubbery.*

> The Senate refused to change a provision that would prohibit taxpayers who do not file itemized returns from deducting charitable contributions.

Readers could probably understand that, or at least they could decipher it without great pain. But we have to present our material so it causes no pain at all. We have to move our full verb phrase, *prohibit from deducting,* over to the neighborhood of *taxpayers.* No problem: *The Senate refused to change a provision that would prohibit taxpayers from deducting charitable contributions if they did not file itemized returns.* Sometimes we rearrange the words, and sometimes we have to get new ones. Always we have to think.

> Researchers said that women of childbearing age in the United States who cannot have children fit a distinct statistical pattern.

The words *in the United States* intrude. We can put them at the end, or we can say that *American women of childbearing age who cannot have children fit a distinct statistical pattern.* We do not have to put *fit* next to *women,* because we are using a full phrase, *women of childbearing age who cannot have children.*

This differs from the hard-freeze example. In that one, the

words right after the noun (*in January and February*) were not a necessary part of the main term, *freeze.* Those words did not limit the freeze. They just told us when the freeze came. You could argue that *taxpayers who did not file itemized returns* is a single term, like *women of child-bearing age.* You're right, but the verb, *prohibit,* needs to be kept close to its other part, *from deducting.* So we move the words around a little, more out of a search for clarity than a desire to follow a rule.

Indeed, rules do not prescribe an all-purpose cure for sentences whose parts won't stay together. Some sentences can be improved with one approach, and some with another. You have to choose the approach that works best. Generally, we just get the modifying clause next to the modified item, as said, and the rest comes easy.

Got all that? Good. Now we can do our regular chores. We can go out and throw the cow over the fence some hay.

# Downtrodden Irregular Verbs

Newspaper writers often run into trouble with irregularity.

I refer to the kind that can be helped by a good memory, not the kind that brings smiles to bran tycoons and Metamucil pushers.

You know: irregular verbs.

They can kill (kill, killed, killed) a good writer. They give us a sinking (sink, sank, sunk/sunken) feeling. They make us want to lie (lie, lay, lain) down to rest or go hang (hang, hanged, hanged) our grammar school teacher.

*Kill* and *hang* do not qualify as irregular verbs. The others do, and they and their friends trouble us. (Well, *hang* goes irregular in one use. You hang a picture, and then you have hung it.)

Time out for definitions. Regular verbs form the past tense and past participle by adding *d* or *ed.* Irregular verbs don't; they indicate past tense and past participle with a vowel change (*swam, swum*) or some other (*broke, broken; blew, blown*). The addition of *n* or *en* is common.

*Lie* and *lay* require special attention, for the words have some overlap. You have *lie, lay* and *lain* as intransitive verbs (*I lie there, I lay there, I had lain there*), and *lay, laid* and *laid* as transitive verbs (*I will lay the book on the table, I laid the book on the table, I have laid the book on the table*). This one gets further complicated by the word *lie,* which means to tell a falsehood. The forms of that regular verb are *lie, lied,* and *lied.* And we might as well note that *lay* has a sexual connotation, too, both as noun and verb.

*Sit* and *set* get in on the fight, too. We have an intransitive *sit,* as in *I sit, I sat, I had sat.* The transitive version is used in *I will set it on the ledge, I set it on the ledge* and *I have set it on the ledge.*

That gets us to newspaper people. I recall stammering once when I called a hospitality suite to ask if the people there had finished off the refreshments. My mind warned my tongue – wrongly – not to ask if they had drunk them all up. I was probably thinking about drunk driving, which should be *drunken driving.* But I certainly didn't want to ask if they had drank it. So I groped. Finally the correct question came out: "Have they drunk all the beer?"

We mortals cannot automatically come up with the correct verb all the time. But we can eliminate some of our stammering, or at least our indecision at the keyboard, by reflection and recollection. We can run through lists – you probably need to make your own – of troublesome verbs. I offer some of the common ones. (Those marked with an asterisk will be discussed.)

| *Present tense* | *Past tense* | *Past participle* |
|---|---|---|
| begin | began | begun |
| blow | blew | blown |
| break | broke | broken |
| bring | brought | brought |
| burst | burst | burst |
| choose | chose | chosen |
| come | came | come |
| dive | dived/dove | dived |
| do | did | done |
| draw | drew | drawn |
| drink | drank | drunk* |
| drive | drove | driven |
| eat | ate | eaten |
| fall | fell | fallen |
| fly | flew | flown |
| freeze | froze | frozen |
| get | got | got/gotten |
| know | knew | known |
| ride | rode | ridden |
| lead | led | led |
| prove | proved | proved* |
| run | ran | run |
| see | saw | seen |
| shine | shone/shined | shone/shined* |

| spring | sprang | sprung |
| sing | sang | sung |
| sink | sank | sunk* |
| swim | swam | swum |
| swing | swung | swung |
| take | took | taken |
| tear | tore | torn |
| throw | threw | thrown |
| tread | trod/treaded | trod* |
| wake | waked | waked* |
| wear | wore | worn |
| write | wrote | written |

Let's look at *drunken, proven* and *sunken.* We use the first as an adjective, as in drunken driving. Do not refer to drunk sailors; they are drunken sailors. They can be drunk. They can be drunks. But when the word is followed by a noun or a verbal such as *driving,* we need *drunken.* I bring up *proven* because too many people try to use it as a verb: Copy editors have proven their great value. No. They have *proved* it. But you should note that their work is of *proven* value, using an adjective. Then we have *sunk* and *sunken.* Some women have sunken cheekbones. Pirates used to sink ships. After they had sunk those ships, people searched for sunken treasure.

*Shined* is the proper past tense or past participle for *shine* when it means "to make shiny by polishing." The rest of the time we use *shone.* To wit: *Her face shone with excitement, and she was glad she had shined her shoes.*

*Wake* and *waked* have two nasty first cousins, *awake* and *awaken.* First: *I wake someone, I waked someone, I had waked someone.* Then we must tackle *awake,* which has both transitive and intransitive versions. The transitive: *I awake her every morning, I awoke (or awaked) her yesterday, I had awaked her earlier.* The intransitive: *I awake when the cat wants out, I awoke when the cat leapt off the dresser.* Cousin No. 2, *awaken,* is used like this: *I awaken her daily, I awakened her yesterday, I had awakened her earlier.* Life would be simpler if we had fewer choices. We rarely use *awaked.* You might find it worthwhile to run these through your head in a variety of sentences until you find yourself comfortable with your choices.

We probably ought to touch on *hang* again, if only to remind you of the twin path it takes. *Hanged* refers to people; *hung,* to other objects. *He was hanged for stealing a side of beef that hung in the locker.* *Hung* also has a slang meaning that requires some care in a family newspaper.

Nearby we encounter *tread*. Step lightly around this rascal. We see *trod* used mistakenly far too often, as in: *North High trods on Central.* That's like saying North High *walkeds* on Central; you cannot add an *s* to the past tense. Try *treads* in the headline above. Don't abandon *trod* altogether; it has plenty of legitimate uses as a past tense: *Olivier trod the boards. Hitler trod on Europe.* Finally, remember that we use *trodden* as a past participle in *the well-trodden path.*

I don't think I have ever written a piece more technical than this, probably because I flounder on grammatical fine points. We all flounder. We can minimize the floundering by paying attention as we write, by using the dictionary, by going over our lists and by looking back over our printed work to make sure we either did it right or won't do it wrong next time.

# Don't Be So Negative

Don't quit paying attention, because I want it to be unlikely that you would miss my sermon against not failing to encourage yourself in preventing excessive use of negatives.

If you understand that first sentence, you don't need the sermon.

Actually, most of us need the sermon, or at least we need a reminder to watch out for negatives. They can take all the smoothness out of our communication. The elimination of negatives almost always makes a sentence easier to understand.

We can have a negative sentence without using *no* or *not* or *nor* and their kin. We can easily spot the nons, the N words, but we need to be alert for other kinds of negative statements. They abound. You should give every one of them a sharp look, possibly a cutting look.

This does not mean you should avoid all negative expressions. Indeed, the preceding sentence has one because I know of no way to phrase that thought without a negative. Mainly, though, you should beware of using more than one negative, particularly when they cancel each other.

I see, more often than I like, this ancient construction: *The tournament was not without surprises.* That usually shows up in the copy of someone more interested in sounding like a literary big shot than in communicating. Writers should stay on the clearest path to communication. Any other choice is not unlike folly.

Let's look at some other examples of problems with negatives. People with an interest in writing will find much to chew on in the following sentence:

More than 300 people signed a petition protesting the Brightsville
School District's policy barring students from promotion ceremonies
if they fail to meet academic standards but are nevertheless not held
back from promotion.

This gives us a double dose of negativism. People are *protesting* (meaning they don't like something, and that's our first negative).
They protest a policy that *bars* (another negative) students. The words
*fail to meet, nevertheless,* and *not held back* also contain negatives. This
sentence makes readers work for every ounce of information. Readers
do not like to work that much. Anyway, a reader who puzzles this out
will see that the 300 people want students to go through the ceremony
even though they fall below normal standards. Try this as an easier
way to say that: *More than 300 residents have petitioned the Brightsville
School District to change its mind and allow all students to attend promotion ceremonies if they are promoted, even if they do not meet academic
standards.*

OK, let's look at another newspaper example of rampant negativism:

He disputed the players' statement that they were unable to turn
down the arbiter's offer.

That has three negative elements: *disputed, unable* and *turn
down.* You have to have at least one, because the story tells about a
negative happening, a dispute. But we get an easier-to-swallow version
if we say: *He disputed the players' statement that they had to accept the
arbiter's offer* (if that happens to be accurate).

The House reversed today its vote to disallow the sale of beer at
collegiate football games.

We would be a lot better off without negatives. Maybe: *The
House reversed itself today and said colleges can sell beer at football games.*
That makes a clear statement about what has happened.

Joseph said he does not expect an attempt to prevent the referendum
unless the tax is not rejected.

Tough, isn't it? You cannot edit or rewrite this satisfactorily
without more information, of course. I'll supply it. The facts would

cause us to say something like this: *Joseph said he thinks residents will let the referendum be held unless the tax proposal passes.*

> The Legislature refused to pass Wednesday, on a 70-48 vote, a bill that would have prohibited county employees from organizing opposition to the move.

Note the negative ideas: *refused, prohibited* and *opposition.* You have to have some negatives in this one, as in the others, because the legislature said no. However, we can make it easy on readers by saying something like this: *The Legislature voted 70-48 Wednesday to allow county employees to organize opposition to the move.*

This material has nothing to do with the double negatives your grade school teacher warned you about. You remember: *I don't want no beans.* We can classify that as a grammar problem, as opposed to a problem of general understanding. The same goes for that line from an old Waylon Jennings–Willie Nelson tune: "Out in Luckenbach, Texas, ain't nobody feeling no pain." That one pounds you with a triple negative. Some songwriters mangle the language daily. Shun them.

Songwriters' double negatives do not get into newspapers regularly, though I occasionally see problems in headlines. Here was one, with the problem caused by a tight count: *No bond disturbs attorney.* That says the attorney is not disturbed by any bonds. The writer meant to say the attorney was disturbed by a lack of a bond. Negatives can give you a pain in the head, too.

# 5

# Getting Started Right

Leads: some say nothing, and some say too much  ●  Other
approaches  ●  *Hard news, soft news. First-day, second-day and folo leads.*
Time element: best after the verb  ●  Transitions  ●  Tenses
●  *Agreement required. Some practice on tense*

## Leads: Some Say Nothing, and Some Say Too Much

Let's look at leads and some of the other problems of organiz-
ing a story and getting it to hang together.

Granny, what a bear track! Brother, what a ball game!

Tanner Laine of the *Midland* (Texas) *Reporter-Telegram* wrote
that lead on a basketball game (Stanton 43, Crane 41) in 1947 or 1948.
It lacks something in finesse, it has those wretched exclamation
marks, and it takes too much time to get to the point. I liked it.

That's the first newspaper lead I recall, one from my child-
hood. That makes it memorable, in a way, and newspapers ought to be
giving readers more memorable leads. I would settle for more that are
not so forgettable.

Few of us dispute the thought that the lead outranks all other
paragraphs in importance, but still we get too many weak leads. Why?
Well, first, the clock kills us; we don't have time to polish everything to
a high gloss. Second, we fail to put ourselves in the reader's place; we

know all the facts and forget that readers are being exposed to brand-new information.

Every now and then we get done in by a gremlin, such as the transposition of lines. But that gives us less trouble than the clock.

Let's look at a typical example of the foremost sin in newspaper writing, use of the say-nothing lead:

> Martin Elred spoke to the Lamar High School Marching Band Alumni Association Tuesday night.

That's all. That lead could have been written long before the speech. It says nothing, and readers who have no particular interest in the alumni association may well move on to another story.

If the speaker doesn't come up with some words of wisdom worth reporting, perhaps the whole story should be scrapped. Surely old Elred said that blowing on a tuba will increase longevity or cause early deafness or build character or something.

I had another lead from a plains-state newspaper, but my filing system let it get away. It went something like this, and you have seen its kinfolks many times:

> The Elred County Library Association met Tuesday at the Courthouse for its regular monthly meeting. Clarissa Merganthaler, president, presided.

The story rambled along like that for three paragraphs, telling about the minutes being read and approved and so on, and then it got around to mentioning that the association voted to install a time capsule in a new county building. While news of a time capsule may not cause the earth to tremble, it nevertheless makes a better lead than a simple note that a meeting was held.

You and I know how leads like that get into the newspaper. A member of the association covers the meeting, because the newspaper doesn't have enough reporters to staff everything. The handwritten copy gets to the office just before deadline. The editor wants to run something but doesn't really have time to do the proper polishing. So someone types up the story and sends it to the typesetter, as is.

We all suffer.

Next December, when we reach the time for New Year's resolutions, perhaps we could resolve to do a better job on leads in the remainder of this century. We could resolve to have all our leads say something. We could resolve to use different kinds of leads when we have different kinds of stories. (The plain summary lead remains the workhorse and will take care of 75 percent of your news, but sometimes we need a little variety.) We could resolve to say more in fewer words.

A lead that runs more than 30 words will probably be hard to understand. I consider 30 the normal maximum, with 20 better. Sometimes, I have students write leads of 10 or fewer words. That tends to cut down on flowery phrases.

Let's look at one more offbeat lead, this one a winner on a worm story by Rod Aydelotte of the *Lampasas* (Texas) *Dispatch*:

> They squiggle
> squirm
> wiggle
> twist
> don't bite
> and make money.

Bear in mind that this weird stuff won't do as a steady diet. Plain old summary leads – the straight news leads you may call them – belong on most stories. But even those do not have to be dull. They had better not be, or we lose readers.

We'll go into this subject again with a discussion of second-day leads, folos and whatever else springs to mind.

# Other Approaches
## Hard News, Soft News

Some definitions:

*A first-day lead* provides the first report of a news event, focusing on the immediacy of the event.

*A folo lead* (follow) provides an update on a story already published. It deals with a new angle of a changing story.

*A second-day lead* deals with an aspect used in the first published version of the story but not treated as the lead.

Now, all three kinds can come in *hard news* or *soft news* versions. Do not think you will have a test on this; we schoolteachers use the terms mainly so we can discuss the writer's work. You know all these definitions, though you may use some other terms. That lead on Granny and the bear track, in the previous section, goes under the soft news label. The hard news version of that story would have said:

*Stanton's basketball team beat Crane, 43-41, Thursday night.* Oh, a writer could have embellished that a little, telling of the game's importance or citing some special heroics, but the basic story lies in those eight words. That's the hard news.

Some newspapers stick with the hard news approach on all news stories, though not with features. They take the view that a news event has not been reported until reported by that newspaper. That attitude, if expressed consistently, will get you by. It doesn't recognize reality, but it enables readers to meet the news on the same terms every day, or every week for a weekly publication. Readers can adjust.

Other newspapers go for the softer approach, trying to find an angle different from the one that merely states the facts. Let me make one up for an illustration. We can put it on the basketball story. Remember, this is a soft news, first-day lead:

> Coach Leo Fields changed his lineup for the first time this year Thursday. He replaced two of his tallest basketball players with shorter but quicker guards to counter Crane's renowned speed.
> The move paid off with a 43-41 victory in a battle for the district lead.

Some people call that backing into the lead, rather than going right at it. I would use that approach if I knew an event would have been covered by competing newspapers, and possibly broadcasters, by the time I could publish. It gives the report a twist.

## First-day, Second-day and Folo Leads

But what about our folo and second-day leads? In order to have a folo lead, we have to have some new event, some development in a continuing story. If Crane's coach had protested a call at the game, we would have that down in our original story, probably. Let's say he filed a protest the next day with district officials. We would have a folo lead, a new story, growing out of the original story, run a day earlier. The folo lead thus goes on the follow-up story, not the first story.

Here's a better illustration: Say we have a bank robbery. Our first-day news story says someone robbed the bank. On the second day, or perhaps later in the first, after we have made our initial report, a suspect gets caught. Fine. We do a folo story. We say the police caught a suspect in a bank robbery. We have to go back and touch on the details of the robbery, but we focus on the arrest.

Now let's look at the second-day story, which is less interesting. We have to write this kind of story even though we have no new developments; the event retains enough interest to require continued coverage. Weak reporters will probably start the second-day story about like this: *Police officers covered the eastern half of the city Thursday in a search for a man who robbed the First National Bank on Wednesday.* That focuses on the search, an automatic thing, rather than on the robbery we had already reported.

The second-day lead on our basketball story might note that other District 12 teams found themselves behind a new leader Thursday—or some other secondary angle. The second-day story has an obvious drawback—we must put the lead on an angle, already down in the first story, that was not important enough to be the lead earlier. We have no new news.

Ideally, we would never have a second-day story. Every story would be updated with new information. The coach would say he will stick to the new lineup or will fight the protest or will take a day off and enjoy the victory. We look for something new.

Do not worry if you see little difference between the soft news first-day lead and the second-day lead. However, you must see the difference between those two and the hard news lead, because you have to make decisions. If your newspaper considers an event unreported until it gets into the newspaper, then you go with hard news, first-day material. You must not spring for the softer material before the news has ever been reported. That is, you must not report on the police search before reporting on the robbery, even though the search is more recent, unless you admit that others have covered the news ahead of you.

You have more fun when you report the news first.

# Time Element: Best after the Verb

The time element in a news lead works best somewhere after the predicate.

Like this: *The city council canned the mayor Friday.*

Stick with this basic premise, that the day goes somewhere behind the verb, and you will do a better job most of the time. The day does not have to snuggle up to the verb as the next word, but it should come along fairly soon.

Of course, life gets complicated sometimes, and this preferred positioning will not always work. For example:

Two Supreme Court justices Thursday sharply rebuked subpoenas approved by the House Judicial Affairs Committee, suggest-
ing they were issued to enhance chairman Martin Elred's race for the
Texas House.

When you have multiple clauses and more than one verb or
participle or gerund, as we have here, you run a risk. If we put the date
after *Committee,* we make readers think the subpoenas were approved
Thursday. The story does not say that. We have to go with the early
placement of the time element or rewrite.

Whatever you do, do not rely on broadcasters for advice on
this subject. Broadcasters often use the time element ahead of the
verb. They can get away with that by stressing an element with inflections not available in print. To wit: *The city council Friday chose the
contractor for a new municipal auditorium.* If they stress *city council,*
they can glide right over the time element without bothering listeners.
Those of us who put words on paper can use italic and boldface type,
but not with the same effect as a broadcaster's inflections. (Generally,
you should avoid typographical gimmickry as a way to show emphasis;
proper wording does it better. Sometimes I can't resist, and I throw in
a splash of italics.)

The problem of placement shows up clearly in short sentences. Try these for silliness: *He Friday retired. She today announced
her candidacy. They tomorrow will reveal their plans, they today said.*

Those little fellows offend the eye (and ear) of anyone who has
an acquaintance with the language. Grammatically, however, those vile
sentences commit no greater sin than this one: *Four engineers Friday
confirmed estimates that the cleanup will cost nearly $2 million.* The little
ones stand out as flawed because of their length.

Sometimes you can simply switch the time element to a new
spot. That will not work in our engineer sentence. We need fuller
revision: *Four engineeers said Friday the city is right in its estimate of $2
million for the flood cleanup.* Better: *Four engineers confirmed Friday
that the flood cleanup will cost nearly $2 million.*

We have another option. We can switch tenses. If we use the
present or present perfect tense, we can dispense with the time element, at least in the lead. (The time element must appear somewhere.)
Thus: *Four engineers say* [present tense] *the city is correct in its estimate
of $2 million for flood cleanup.* Or: *Mayor Earl Koonce wants* [present
tense] *the attorney general to investigate the proliferation of bingo games
in Martin County.* Or: *Mayor Earl Koonce has asked* [present perfect

tense] *the attorney general to investigate the proliferation of bingo games in Martin County.*

We could take even one more tack on that last one: *Mayor Earl Koonce is asking the attorney general to investigate. . . .*

You have to let the facts govern your choice. *Wants* will cover you, whether Earl has made any move or is just thinking it over, if he lets us know he does indeed want this. You do better with *has asked,* because that clearly indicates some action. *Is asking* will do in a pinch, but it has a weak verb. With the present tense, you sometimes have to go over your subject twice. That is, we say Earl wants something, and then we need another sentence to say how his craving has manifested itself—he told us or wrote the attorney general or something.

That shows you why the past tense works best in news. It comes right out and tells readers we have something nailed down. However, the other tenses have their place. Indeed, sometimes we want to take away the value of timeliness, or at least to avoid emphasizing it. Other tenses let us duck the time element when we run a story someone else has already had or when we are simply a little late in reporting a story. They also let us avoid using *recently,* which gives us away for having a dated story. (Honesty requires that we cite the actual date somewhere in our story, but it does not compel us to put in the lead.)

Let's look at another sentence with the day before the verb:

> The Jacksonville City Council Tuesday moved ahead with condemnation proceedings that will allow the city to obtain easements for a replacement sewer main in the Mill Creek basin.

Put the date after *ahead.* I don't want to call this a rule, but the date works all right before a preposition, such as *with* or *for.*

> The major political party caucuses Monday night in Colorado County are expected to have good turnouts.

No big complaint. We have ellipsis here, leaving out the words *that will be held* just before the date. Nevertheless, we would have a better sentence with a verb nearer the beginning: *Democrats and Republicans both predict good turnouts at Monday night's county caucuses.*

> Northern Arizonans Thursday spoke against a federal proposal to save the broad-banded water snake at the possible expense of a dam and reservoir.

Some people are Northern Arizonans Thursday and some are Northern Arizonans forever. Write it this way: *Northern Arizonans spoke up Thursday against.* . . .

California State Police on Wednesday were getting ready to close their investigation into why a job counselor killed his boss and then himself.

We did the right thing by inserting *on* to break up the string of capped words. However, we could have made a slightly smoother sentence by putting the time element after *ready.* Try another:

Former major league pitcher Wayne Garland returned to Panama City Wednesday, where he played his junior college baseball in 1969.

This one reads all right down to the comma, though we could use an *on,* as just discussed. The trouble comes with the final clause, which wants to modify the city. Alas, the time intrudes; the clause has to modify whatever it stands next to. So we should move the time element up a little, right after *returned.* End of problem.

To recap: Try to put the time element behind the predicate. If that won't work cleanly, consider present tense or some other. If that seems too slow in getting into the story, use the time before the predicate – with caution.

# Transitions

Schoolteachers and language columnists love to talk about transitions in writing. We carry on about making the story flow and pulling the reader through the story and such things.

I have no quarrel with the basic idea, making our writing smoother, but the discussion usually gets too abstract. I sometimes haul out an analogy to the construction of a building, using stone (words) and mortar (transitions) rather than straw and dirt. That's just schoolteacher talk. I'll try to come up with something you can work with, some way to use transitions.

Ideally, readers would never notice a transition device. Readers would go from one section of a story to the next, from one paragraph to paragraph, sentence to sentence, even word to word smoothly.

That doesn't happen. Too many of us use abrupt transitions, changing subjects faster than the reader's eye can follow. The writer can follow the shift because the writer already knows the story. Have pity on the reader. Give the reader a hand as you go through the material. String your work together so it makes a continuous narrative, rather than a collection of unrelated paragraphs.

Repetition of a word (or synonym) can tie two thoughts—two paragraphs—together. Likewise, you get a good link by having a figure in one paragraph comment on something from the preceding paragraph. You can even get a good tie with a conjunction, such as *and* and *but,* though you should be careful about overuse.

Let's look at some of these links.

> Elred spent 40 years teaching grammar. He made it his crusade, and for his efforts he suffered many a bloodletting, many a setback, many a defeat. Still, he held high his escutcheon: "Subject, predicate, object," he intoned. Then, in the style of a cheerleader, he shouted, "Go, grammar, go!"
>
> Grammar did not go far with Elred's son. Or maybe it went and didn't come back.

That second paragraph moves readers to a discussion of the son's views. (Don't ask about the boy; I made this one up as I went along, and our story ends right there.) We can do the same thing with our second method, involving comment from the new paragraph. Use the same long first paragraph we had above. Then try this for a transition:

> Elred's son shares none of this enthusiasm for the language.

You may not consider that a comment. It is, though perhaps only indirectly. Perhaps you expected a quotation as the method of comment. No luck. If making a transition, you should not start the second paragraph with a quotation, because we end the first paragraph with one. You should not change speakers without some warning. Far too many readers will overlook the close-quote marks and will think Elred Senior is still talking. Make your changeover to Junior clear. Then support that with a quotation, like this:

> Elred's son shares none of this enthusiasm for the language. "I have no time to fight that foolish battle," he said disdainfully but in perfect English.

Perfect English gets a bruising occasionally when we try our third kind of transition, the conjunction. However, it can work. Some people still object to beginning sentences or paragraphs with conjunctions, but grammarians have generally dropped their prohibition. An example:

> Elred likes biscuits much more than toast. "They have more heft to them, more body. They satisfy you," he said. "I don't think I could get through the week if I had to start with toast every day. I don't like it."
> But he ate it.

You could say the same thing in other ways with about the same effect. Maybe: *He ate it anyway.* Or: *His dislike did not keep him from eating four pieces.*

Actually, I'm not trying to encourage you to use conjunctions as openers. You ought to look hard at them every time. Frequently, you will find them unnecessary. Let's check a couple of useless conjunctions thrown in as sentence starters:

> The Cowboys are trying to repair Elger's ego. "You're fighting for Pat Thomas' spot in the Pro Bowl," Landry told him as they passed in the corridor. "You can do it. You can do it."
> But Elger isn't so sure, and he isn't so sure the Cowboys needed to retool their secondary.

The contrast would be just as evident without the *but.* Read it that way in your mind.

> The sound of purebreds and quarterhorses thundering out of the starting gates is familiar to Boerne rancher Frank Sultenfuss. After all, he has been working the Kendall County Fair races for three decades.
> And it's a sound lots of people from San Antonio, New Braunfels and Fredericksburg have heard, too, because Sultenfuss says he sees the same people year after year in Boerne during the Labor Day weekend races.

The conjunction contributes nothing here either. Indeed, both examples would be better off without the conjunction.

Some other words (such as *however, previously, in conclusion, for instance, nevertheless* and *therefore*) have the same built-in problems that *and* and *but* offer. Writers building sturdy literary works avoid starting paragraphs with these devices, leaving the opening of a paragraph for an element of emphasis.

Reporters do not have time to erect a literary edifice in every story. They are going to come up with the occasional mud hut. But if they get in the habit of using good materials, of using stone and mortar instead of straw and dirt, their structures will stand.

# Tenses

## Agreement Required

This lead showed up on my desk not long ago. Note the tenses:

Customers who tap into Blanktown's water and sewer system in 1987 would have to pay 10 times the current fee if the city's new council adopts a schedule now being considered.

Most of us see right away that we need to do something to that sentence. The writer probably chose *would* on the grounds that *will* sounds so definite. *Would* carries the conditional with it; it has the big *if* built in—we would if we could. However, the sentence already handles the *if* angle straight on. That is, it says something will happen *if* the council acts. So the *would* should be *will.*

Tense problems bother all of us.

Let's go to square one in a discussion of the choice of tense.

The first rule: The tense of the predicate in the independent clause governs the tense of the predicate in the dependent clause.

Therefore: *The governor said he would sign the bill.* You cannot go wrong if you stick to that idea. When in doubt, follow it.

Unfortunately, the trail sometimes leads to a little duller writing than we like. I hate to urge you to break such a good rule, but on occasion you get a better sentence if you do. Try this:

The governor said West Texas has a lot of sand.

I call the statement about West Texas sand an eternal verity, and you should give it the present tense—*has* a lot of sand—despite the rule.

Similarly: *The governor said he will sign the bill next week.* We call that the dynamic tense; it indicates some life, something coming up, something in the future.

We have some pitfalls, of course. Writing wouldn't be any fun if we didn't have pitfalls; it would be too easy.

Take this sentence: *He said the union is* [or *was*] *trying to make non-union hands pawns for contracts they do not* [or *did not*] *want.* Your choice of verbs depends on the circumstances. If our speaker refers to an action that took place yesterday, some specific event that started and stopped, we need the past tense in both places. On the other hand, if our speaker refers to something the union is doing every day, then and now and probably tomorrow, we clearly get a better sentence, a livelier sentence, with present tense.

Let's look at a case in which a shift in tenses is proper even under the rule:

> Although he filled his own high school report card with C's and D's, Gibson now lectures with as much pomposity as anyone.

We make the change to show chronology. We don't find that flow of chronology in this next one:

> Frankie is a dreamer, and no amount of pleading was going to change him.

Readers have nothing but the verbs to help them understand this sentence, and the verbs do an inadequate job.

I took that last example from a book I would like to recommend: *When Words Collide,* by Lauren Kessler and Duncan McDonald of the University of Oregon. You ought to read it. The book makes a handy reference tool. It lacks the detail of my standby, Prentice-Hall's *Handbook for Writers,* but the writing is easier to swallow. You might make reading both those books part of next year's self-improvement project.

They will help you relax in tense situations.

## Some Practice on Tense

You no doubt want some more examples. Fine. Take these. Spot the problem and change it mentally or with a pen.

> The company would sign a lease agreement if the building is brought up to its specifications within a certain time frame.

The company *would* sign if the building *were* brought up. The company *will* sign if the building *is* brought up. And let's scrap *frame.*

> Any athlete who fails to submit to the urinalysis or tests positive for illegal drugs at least two times would not be allowed to participate. . . .

Awkward and needless shift of tenses. Use *will* instead of *would.*

> The girls' softball team at North Montgomery has come a long way since the first game of the year, but it wasn't quite enough.

Be careful in switching tenses. The shift throws readers off. Say the team *came* a long way after the first game, but it wasn't quite enough. *Has come* keeps things alive; use it for something that started in the past and is still happening.

> Whether Goforth Academy keeps its elementary school facilities is up to a chancellor after a two-day hearing ended Wednesday.

The switch in tenses, from present to past, makes this a little rough. We could say the decision was left up to a chancellor after a two-day hearing ended Wednesday. Or we could have done this: *A two-day hearing on whether Goforth Academy keeps its elementary school has left the decision up to a chancellor.*

> Stressed at several points of the MPO meeting last week is the availability of participation for smaller MPO communities through intersection improvements.

First, note the verb tense. We need to use past tense: *Stressed . . . was.* Then let's turn this backward sentence around. (That recalls the comment about *Time* magazine: "Backward ran sentences until reeled the mind.") We want to say something like this: *Officials at last week's MPO meeting frequently stressed the availability of participation for smaller MPO communities through intersection improvements.* Actually, I think this sentence should say: *Officials at last week's MPO meeting frequently stressed that smaller communities can get MPO money to improve intersections.*

Councilman Frank Willis will not say how he would vote if the council takes up a no-confidence motion.

Don't use *would* and *takes*. Make both the same tense: *Councilman Frank Willis will not say how he will vote if the council takes it up.* Or: *Councilman Frank Willis won't say how he would vote if the council took it up.* You could even write: *Councilman Frank Willis wouldn't say how he would vote if the council took it up.*

That chance may never had come if Lewis had not gotten hurt.

Way off. It *might never have come.* You simply use past tense (*might*) when referring to the past, and present (*may*) when referring to now or the future. You also use *might* for some conditionals, as in: *He might relent if he were given a second chance.*

If the elementary school is cut, the junior high would be retained.

Align those tenses. If one *is* cut, the other *will* be retained.

# 6

# Quote, Unquote

Attribution • *When. Where. How.* Handling quotations • *The mechanics. Partial quotes.* Verbatim quotes • Workingman's curse • "Shut up," he explained • Some attribution practice

## Attribution

Let's go into the attribution business.

We deal with attribution every day. Most stories involve interviews or at least some outside source. We have to tell readers which information is from the interview subject or document or whatever. That's attribution.

Attribution problems are split three ways. In order of difficulty, those are *when, where* and *how.* We'll tackle the toughie first.

### When

Here's a lead:

The administration has decided to cut meat imports from Argentina in half Jan. 15, the president announced Monday.

You do not really need the attribution (*the president announced*) in this one. You may—may, not must—drop it when the speaker has the authority to carry out the action implied in the statement. If the president needed congressional approval, things would be different. But if he has the power to cut imports himself, we can end the sentence at

*Jan. 15.* We will of course tell readers, probably in the second paragraph, that the decision came from the White House. We could use the attribution in the first paragraph, and it would lend a little more authority. But we do not really have to use it.

Here's another:

> Meat imports will be cut in half Jan. 15, the White House announced Monday.

I might be tempted to go ahead and use the attribution on this. The sentence is quite short, and the attribution rounds it out.

What I am saying is that we do not have any rules chiseled in stone to guide us on some of these things. You, as a writer or editor, have to make up your mind, basing your judgment on how your readers will perceive the statement.

We can also drop the attribution if the speaker is giving us an eternal verity. The most famous such case is from a filler: *The moon is 239,000 miles from Earth, according to the Associated Press.*

If the fact is widely accepted, it does not need attribution. (For that matter, if it is so well known, it may not belong in the lead. Also, the moon's distance from Earth varies, but that is another subject.)

A first cousin to the eternal verity is the easily verifiable fact. For instance:

> Nevawin High School has scheduled its first nine-game football season in 20 years, Coach Martin Elred announced Monday.

While it may massage Coach Elred's ego to see his name high in the story, that attribution is not necessary. You can easily verify that the Fighting Wasps have only nine games, and your library will tell you how many years they have been playing 10. Later in the story you will mention Coach Elred, probably as early as the second paragraph, with a quote. Meanwhile, you can tighten your lead by leaving out an attribution that is not needed.

When *do* you need attribution?

Well, normally you need it with a statement of opinion or a fact that the reader cannot verify or accept on faith. Let's write a new second paragraph for our Fighting Wasps story. Remember that we cut the attribution from the lead, so we aren't repeating Elred's name:

> The Wasps will be small but slow, Coach Martin Elred said. They should win six or seven of the nine games, he said.

I could go along with an unattributed assessment of size, since that is easily measurable. I would hesitate to have the newspaper assess speed, though we might do it if the team was outstandingly fast or slow. But the victory prediction definitely requires attribution. Lay it off on the coach. Don't take the back door approach: *Experts rate the Wasps as favorites to beat everyone but Sundown and Seagraves on their short schedule.* Those experts are usually you and the coach and maybe the *Daily News* guy who came by and talked to the coach a week ago.

Let me summarize: Use attribution on any statement of opinion and on statements of facts that are not readily verifiable. You do not have to attribute eternal verities, easily obtainable facts or predictions by people who have the power and authority to carry out those predictions.

## Where

OK. Now, where do you put attribution?

Three choices: beginning, middle, end. Middle usually works best. End finishes a close second. Beginning is last. Do not throw us a string of paragraphs or sentences beginning with *Elred said.* Put the attribution in the most natural, most unobtrusive spot. The reader should glide right over it. Try one. Where in the next sentence would you put *the mayor said?*

"The sign is here. It's just a matter of what words they put on it."

I would put it after *here.* There you have a natural break. You could go to the end, and putting it at the beginning is not wrong. But the natural break, the middle, is the best spot. Good writers learn to move words around mentally before making the final editing decision. Think it over. Then act.

## How

We are left with only the how in our basic trio. Easy job. By far the best word for attribution is *said.* It is safe, neutral, bland. It gives no opinion.

It does not carry any of the precision of *admitted, charged, contended, added, mentioned* and *noted.* Those words have a place. When you want to tell about the mayor admitting something, you choose *admitted.* You must be careful, of course, because the mayor may just be saying something, not admitting it. If you say the mayor admitted he had not seen the bridge plans, you imply that the mayor should have seen them. When *admitted* is the right word, use it. Otherwise, fall back on *said.*

Use *stated* twice a week, *declared* in odd months, *opined* on July 4 of a leap year and *averred* on your 90th birthday.

Even if you already know more about attribution than you really want to know, you need to think about the subject. Make decisions consciously, for your choice of position has an effect on readability. This is a moderately complex but sort of interesting subject. Work on it.

# Handling Quotations
## The Mechanics

Quotations give us other problems. Some people have trouble with the mechanics – where to put the marks and the attribution. Some have trouble with the logic – when to use quotation marks. Some have other problems.

Let's look at mechanics first. You know where the opening quotation marks go. No problem. The closing marks come in when you stop quoting. If you throw in a *he said,* you have to close the quotation before the attribution and reopen it afterward to continue a quotation. If the words were not uttered by the speaker, they do not go between quotation marks.

If you carry a quotation over from one paragraph to another, you do not close the quotation at the end of the first paragraph. You open the next paragraph with quotation marks.

The comma and period always go inside the quotation marks. The semicolon and colon go outside. The question mark's spot depends. Let's say you write this: *Is this the famous "tiger's paw defense"?* The quotation is not the complete question, just part of it, so the question mark goes outside. More often, you will write something like this: *He asked, "Where will it end?"* In that case, your full quotation is a question, so the quotation marks embrace the question mark, too.

Now for attribution. We have clear rules here. Next to, or within, every direct quotation, you must have attribution. A *she said* at the end of one paragraph will carry over to the next when the quotation continues. The same goes for sentences. Not every individual paragraph of a long, uninterrupted quotation has to have attribution, but you must have it somewhere in the string. (It generally goes best at the first natural break. Put it at the end if you find no natural break. A quotation of more than one paragraph would require attribution in the first paragraph.) Put it at the beginning for certain effects, such as for variety and for clarity when switching between two speakers.

If the quotation is interrupted by an unquoted sentence, you must have attribution again after you renew the quoting. However, if you merely break a quotation for attribution and an extra clause — a short clause — you do not have to have new attribution. Example: *"These guys are slothful," said Jones, their foreman. "I could do twice as much without them."* Attribution is acceptable with the second sentence, but you can get by without it. If you had a longer sentence or a paragraph after *their foreman,* you would be wise to add enough attribution to remind readers who was talking.

The word *said* does the best job in neutral attribution. Use it most of the time. Use others only when called for. (These could be all right: *"Help me," she pleaded. "Stop it," he shouted. "I'll try," she whispered.*) Watch out for excessive pomp. (*"I'll go," he stated. "We ought to put on a show," she declared. "I will always support the union," he averred.*) Be doubly wary of the weird ones. (*"I like that," he grinned. "That hurts," he grimaced. "You'll get over it," he chuckled.*)

Be alert, too, when moving between people doing the speaking. Hurried writers sometimes change speakers with inadequate warning. They end a quotation from one source and immediately start a new quotation from some other source, one who occasionally offers exactly the opposite opinion from the first speaker's. They give you no warning stronger than tiny closing quotation marks. Readers overlook those marks, or if the material ends with a *Smith said,* they think the new quotation is a continuation from the same person. Then they wonder what has happened because the speaker appears to be contradicting himself.

The solution: Be clear in introducing new speakers. Instead of ending with a quotation from Jones and then starting with one from Smith, give us a signal. Like this: *Smith disagreed with the plan. "This has no merit," he said.*

What about paraphrases? Beginners sometimes see an attribution (*She said*) and assume that whatever follows is a direct quote. Not so. Well, not necessarily so. You can use a direct quote without marks and call it a paraphrase. More often, the paraphrase is used to show the gist of a person's remarks, especially with long-winded or jargon-spouting speakers. Take this quotation for example: *"We believe that the hardworking faculty members of this magnificent educational institution should be the recipients of increased financial rewards accompanied by a sharp lessening of onerous job-related tasks," Elred said.* Paraphrase it: *Elred said the faculty should have more pay and less work.*

## Partial Quotes

Sometimes we want to use only the kernel of a statement, a partial quotation, rather than the full statement. Partial quotations let us strip out verbiage and retain some of the flavor of the speaker. A caveat: The use of a single quoted word or short term by itself can cause confusion. Example: *He said the project was a "rip-off."* Readers have to guess whether the speaker or the writer produced that quoted word. If the speaker used it, the writer should supply enough of the original wording to make the origin clear. In this case, just the word *a* before *rip-off* would indicate that the term came from the speaker, not the writer. If the speaker said, for example, that the project was *"an absolute rip-off,"* such a longer term in quotes would make that clear.

Many writers reach for the quotation marks when they use slang on their own. They mean to indicate they know better than to use the pedestrian language of their readers. They err. The quotation marks imply that the writer knows he or she is stooping, but the writer thinks the reader, being an inferior person, will not recognize slang. Rule: If you want to use slang or specialized terms, write without apology, without quotation marks to call attention to the oddity. If the term is so odd that you feel you need the marks, find another term. I don't want to sound "hard-nosed" about this, but it "chaps" me to see writers who don't give a "hoot."

And then we have the partial quote that leads into a longer quote. When you have a partial quotation, covered by one verb, you need to close the quotation marks and open a new quotation, with new attribution, for a continued thought.

In one I saw recently, the original two sentences probably read like this: *Jones said, "In the year I knew him, Bob Smith became my best friend. I wish I had met him earlier."* That came out in the newspaper this way: *Jones called Smith his "best friend. I wish I had met him earlier."*

Even though the words *best friend* immediately precede the full sentence as part of the original quotation, the writer took liberties with that sentence, and it can no longer be considered part of a string. The words *best friend* are covered by a different verb; they should have their own quotation marks.

To summarize: Every quotation has to touch attribution, at least indirectly. Writers must give clear signals when they change speakers in a string of quotations. Long-winded or flowery statements can usually be reduced to paraphrases with benefits to all. Partial quotes can be helpful, but single-word quotations are dangerous. Slang and jargon should not be quoted in apology. A partial quote cannot supply the verb of attribution for a full sentence that follows.

# Verbatim Quotes

Almost all of us say we want to report quotations verbatim. Almost all of us admit we cannot quite do that. Almost all of us clean up some lapses in a speaker's utterances.

And there we run into problems.

The word *verbatim* is the first casualty in a discussion about quotations. Newspapers rarely use anything verbatim, meaning "in exactly the same words." A verbatim report would include all the minor lapses of grammar, all the *you knows* and all the mispronunciations, not to mention profanity.

No one wants such a statement, so we clean things up.

We tidy up after people who bite off their *g*'s, as in *I'm goin' to be doin' some singin' at the beginnin' of the program.* I see no harm in sticking the *g*'s on those words. The act does not mislead readers. Readers will not boggle even if they read our words and immediately hear the words spoken in a broadcast.

On the other hand, if a speaker says "He's a veritable tower of pusillanimity," and we quote him as saying "That guy has no guts," the difference will be startling enough to catch a reader's eye, though the sentences mean the same thing.

Of course, we need some goal other than trying not to get caught playing around with quotes. In using quotations, we try to give both the exact wording and the exact meaning. Actually, the reporter's job requires even more. The exact wording and the exact meaning have to be in a tighter package than the one the speaker offered. We cannot just become conduits and relay six or seven paragraphs of quotation, forcing readers to extract the meaning and supply perspective.

Such lengthy quotation would shift the burden to the speaker, but it would hurt readers. They would have to wade through a mass of verbiage to get the kernel of meaning that reporters are paid to supply.

The good writer uses quotations to support the narrative, not to carry it. Therefore, reporters are obliged to sift the meaning from a sea of quotes to help readers. Reporters must condense quotes into a meaningful arrangement of unquoted material—paraphrase—and use the key quote to support the main point. An example: *Nixon said the idea of a comeback has some appeal. "I sort of like the limelight," he told the editors.*

In that one, the former president spent a few minutes discussing a political comeback. The reporter summarized Nixon's views—the idea has appeal. Then the reporter used a quotation to illuminate the reasoning.

Fine. Well done. But that doesn't tell us what to do with people who murder the language, especially those offbeat characters who frequently show up in newspaper features. If we want to give the flavor of some people, we have to quote their lapses. Listen to a Cajun: *Somebody done shut you gate wide open and let all you cows dat was in de pasture out.* Lovely. Try that in straight English and you lose all the flavor. (Be careful not to sound condescending when quoting those who don't have your linguistic background. And be aware that you will probably botch the job if you try dialect. I got my Cajun sentence from a Cajun.)

You can also lose the flavor with improper quotes in an interview with someone like William F. Buckley Jr. If you see three Buckley sentences with no terms like *pusillanimous* or *inordinately obfuscatory*, you know the reporter changed the quotations. You have to capture people like Buckley with their precise words. But if the reporter does nothing but quote Buckley, readers get chopped up by that broadsword vocabulary. Reporters should decipher most of Buckley's language, putting it into English for regular readers. The occasional quote provides illumination or emphasis.

Now and then, however, you have an ignoramus in public office and you want readers to see what kind of jerk he is. Be careful. If you quote him as saying "Them fool guys ain't got no bidness testificating afore the gran' jury," you should do so with forethought. Fairness requires that you treat everyone the same in news stories. You will have trouble responding to the sinner just cited if he accuses you of making him out as a fool while you clean up the grammar of his political opponents.

On the other hand, you have some obligation to show readers what their public servants are like, especially if these people do not get much broadcast exposure.

A dilemma.

I would suggest a straightforward assault. Go right at the offender. Do a story about his casual acquaintance with the language. First, ask readers whether it bothers them. Find out whether people know what the fellow is like. Get a list of his pithiest sayings. Collect the best stuff from past notes and from six months of observation. Then lay it out. (Don't do this unless you believe his grammar reflects his intelligence rather than his education, and unless that in turn reflects on his ability to perform his duties.)

Oh. You say he's profane, too. That adds a problem. I would suggest the straightforward approach here, too, with a twist. Simply tell this person — and all other sources — that you have to quote exact language when it's pertinent. Do not go out of your way to find a quote with profanity in it, but let officials know they will be held accountable for what they say. How you put the language into the newspaper — with blips or dashes or whatever — is up to you. I believe you ought to use it straight, but only if the quotation illustrates a point. That is, instead of changing Jimmy Carter's quote to "I'll whip his fanny," I would tell readers exactly what Carter once said about Ted Kennedy, if I thought the idea needed to be reported. That one did, of course.

My answers do not fit everyone. Find your own. Think about them. Talk about them. The problem of accurate quotation will be with us for a long time, and you may as well decide how you want to handle it.

# Workingman's Curse

We continue our discussion of profanity and obscenity. I don't know how to discuss strong language completely without using the words under discussion. So I will use two, in context, scientifically, with the laboratory approach.

The subject arose in two newspapers I read. In one, the *Delta Democrat-Times* of Greenville, Miss., the editor wrote a column about a politician who had a suggestion for the editor. "Kiss my ass" was the quaint way he put it. This brassy politician made his remark, more than once, at a party put on by the newspaper. Not only that, he then said the editor didn't have the guts to run the quotation.

He guessed wrong. The editor, despite awareness of his Bible Belt surroundings, ran the quote in a column poking fun at the politician. He attributed his own decision to foolhardiness rather than courage. He noted, too, that he could not oblige the politician because the state's laws forbade such activity.

The editor, a friend, asked my view. You're getting it.

I would have run the quotation, though with some fear, on the grounds that people have a right to see the warts on their public servants. I would certainly try to handle it with humor, as the *DD-T* editor did, rather than making it sound as if the politician had committed an offense worthy of impeachment. Hypocrisy does not make an editor look good. So the editor didn't thunder about the vileness of this person; he merely said this is how the guy talks, even when his mouth is full of someone else's food.

The editor worried, as he should have, but he got no adverse mail. People probably sided with the editor when the politician said the editor was afraid to tell the people the words being used.

We have all heard that expression, so no one would be truly shocked.

However, newspapers elevate their language just a little, not enough so regular people can't understand it but enough to get out of the muck. And that means we set up a policy that forbids the use of profanity and obscenity most of the time.

I would use strong language only in a quotation, and then only if the quotation was pertinent to the understanding of something significant. As I noted a few paragraphs ago, I would not hesitate to report that President Carter said he would whip Ted Kennedy's ass, or that George Bush, at debate time, said he was going out to kick some ass.

Those people, major government figures, used the words. I am not trying to punish them. I just want to make sure people know what the fuss is about, if we have a fuss.

Remember Earl Butz? I would have run the quotation that cost him his job as secretary of agriculture. He said blacks want nothing but good sex, loose shoes and a warm place for bodily functions. (He offered that view in earthier language.) You ought not rerun the quotation on Page 1 every day, but the readers are entitled to know what a person could possibly say that would get him kicked out of one of the nation's top jobs.

Let's turn now to the other side, when you would excise blue language.

The *Orange County Register,* of Santa Ana, Calif., had letters of complaint because it quoted a rock musician as saying something had pissed him off.

I would not have used his quote. I admit some rock stars make more money than cabinet members. Nevertheless, their utterances are seldom of as much importance in the course of the republic. They certainly were not significant in the article cited.

So the editor reminded staffers, through an ombudsman column, that the *Register* has a firm, written policy. The policy makes sense. It says, basically, that you do not run gratuitous profanity or obscenity. Unless it is necessary to the understanding of an important story—note the words *necessary* and *important*—it doesn't run. You do not have to rewrite quotations; you just paraphrase the speaker and drop out the bad words. Oh, I could accept an occasional absolute deletion. Example: *I have a dirty, lousy, stinking, fucking job.* I would not question the intellectual honesty of an editor who deleted *fucking*. Deletion would not ruin the story's integrity. But paraphrasing is better, as is a partial quote.

Anyway, every newspaper ought to write down its policy. All of us should think about the problem. We do not need to offend anyone without reason, and dirty language will indeed offend some people. But we must make sure our readers fully comprehend the news.

# "Shut Up," He Explained

The city editor beckoned the reporter to his desk. "Scoop," he growled, "I want to talk to you about attribution. You're using the wrong words."

"Hey, look, it's not my fault," Scoop whined. "I'm only doing what I see others do. You want something different, just let me know, Ed," he groveled.

"You mean you don't know any better?" Ed questioned.

"If I knew any better I would advise you," Scoop related.

"This is ridiculous," Ed responded. "You have to get on the ball or hit the road," he asserted.

"Right," agreed Segundo, the assistant at Ed's elbow. "You better shape up or ship out," he cliched.

"You sure you mean that?" the reporter questioned. "Jeez. I'm not sure I can use all those strange words you like," he mumbled.

"Do it!" the editor thundered. "We can find someone else who wants the job," he harrumphed. "Either get attribution straight or take a hike," he remonstrated.

"All right," the reporter toadied, "but I'd like to have a couple of weeks to practice."

"I'll give you a week," the editor scowled, "and then we find someone else."

"You're a tough one, boss," the assistant marveled.

"Thanks, kid," he blushed.

"You're an inspiration for all of us," Segundo worshiped.

"I'll go along with that," Scoop concurred.

"Knock off the bull lather and get back to work, both of you," the editor grumped.

"You bet, boss," the reporter chirped. He brightened. "I think I'll go tell the other reporters about your new policy," he grinned.

"Good lad," the editor praised.

"He'll go far—he's got moxie," Segundo gushed as the reporter left.

"I don't think so," Ed contradicted. "He has some self-doubts he has to get rid of before he will be where he should," he analyzed.

"Maybe," Segundo doubted, "but you could be right. What do you see as his writing weaknesses?"

"Lack of variety in his vocabulary," Ed pinpointed. "Do you read his stuff carefully?" he queried. "The kid knows only one verb of attribution."

Segundo frowned. "I can't believe that," he dissented. "I hadn't really noticed," he admitted. "He must not read much."

"That's my guess," Ed opined. "I don't suppose he has ever heard of Ring Lardner."

"Why Lardner?" Segundo puzzled.

"Lardner gets my vote for one passage, a bit of dialogue reading, ' "Shut up," he explained.' "

"Do you think you have the quote marks right in that last sentence?" Segundo inquired.

"Don't worry about the quote marks. Worry about the verbs," Ed ordered.

"You know, boss," Segundo broached, "I've been meaning to ask about a verb I saw in the opposition."

"Yes?" Ed demanded.

"Maybe you've heard it somewhere. It's called *say*," he muttered.

"That's all we need," Ed fumed. "Somebody wants to bring in a simple verb," he sputtered. "They have no respect for tradition," he stormed. "Next they'll want to do away with my old typewriter," he crescendoed.

He calmed.

"They'll never change me," he chortled.

"How's that, boss?" Segundo interrogated.

"Variety is the spice of life," he axiomed.

"You're right again boss," Segundo flattered. "You have all the answers, if I may aver so myself."

# Some Attribution Practice

"Well," justified 6-year-old Tiffany Potter as she gobbled up the last of her homemade necklace, "I was just hungry."

Not a good verb of attribution. She *said* that. Or try this: *"Well, I was just hungry," 6-year-old Tiffany Potter said in telling why she ate her homemade necklace.* Note that the original separated *Well* from the rest of the quote with 16 words.

"It's a shame to play 80 games and have what should be an all-time record spoiled by three rotten calls," Sharman, ever the perfectionist, burned.

Another bad verb. You might get away with *fumed Sharman, ever the perfectionist.* But that *burned* has to stand in line behind a lot of other words that have not yet earned respectability in attribution.

Ballard, who has three grown children, has worked for the district for 22 years. "Having to be away from your children takes something out of you. The first concern of most women is their families. But society has changed, and families need two incomes."

We have to guess who said that. Every quotation must touch attribution at some point. The touch can be tenuous—two or three paragraphs away, as long as the quotation is uninterrupted. Sometimes you can clearly indicate attribution with a colon. However you do it, you must attribute every quotation.

"We're already getting great information," said Kraai, "on why fish do things at different times."

The attribution interrupted the flow of the quote. We could read the first clause as an entity: *We're already getting great information.* But that was only half the story. Put the attribution at the end.

"You really have your work cut out for you," Benes says with a laugh, "if you want to have a successful marriage."

Same problem. The attribution makes us think the first clause is a complete sentence. It interrupts the thought.

The organization's first planned activity will take place during Arboretum Awareness Week, Zohman said, which begins Sept. 29, to promote the facility on the Cal State Fullerton campus.

Get the *which* clause next to *Week,* which it modifies. Put the attribution at beginning or end of the sentence; we don't have a good place in the middle.

# 7

# Editor's Outlook

Looking for flaws • *Levels of editing. Wanted: editors.* Ten timely tips: things an editor should know—and do • Statistics • Five questions for users of statistics • A statistical quiz

## Looking for Flaws
### Levels of Editing

I suspect that almost everyone who reads this sterling publication does some copy editing. Most of you would no doubt do more if you had time.

You can save a little time by cultivating a copy editor's mentality. This mentality tells you to look at all copy, your own included, with an eye toward simplification, with an intention of cutting the unnecessary.

The saving of time comes when you do things automatically—when, for example, you have deleted three words from *at the corner of 26th and Guadalupe* so often that you quit writing *the corner of.* People know that two streets have a corner (or *the intersection of*). The words only take up space.

These words come out at the lowest level of editing—the *word* level. There we either cut words or replace phrases with single words. *Educational facilities* become *schools. Members of ethnic minorities* become *blacks and Hispanics. A small number of* becomes *few. In the near future* becomes *soon. At the present time* becomes *now. A great number of times* becomes *often.* And *people prominent in the field of newspaper editing* become *prominent editors,* or just *editors.*

Editing has a second level. This one involves your willingness and ability to look at a piece of copy and see how a sentence could be drastically revised by changing only a few words, as opposed to a full rewrite. On this level, we develop habits of trying to make every sentence carry as much freight as we can get on it and still be clear. Clear. Clear. Always clear. We look for different, usually shorter, ways to say things. Example:

> The deepwater port they proposed to build would handle only crude oil, sending it to tank farms on the shore through a system of pipelines.

Change that to this:

> Their proposed deepwater port would handle only crude oil, piping it to tank farms ashore.

Two thoughts here: 1. *To build* can frequently be inferred; all structures have to be built or erected or put up before they exist. 2. More important, this bit about sending something through pipelines has many counterparts if we look for the right verbs. Instead of coming out against something in an editorial, we editorialize against it. Instead of giving someone a starting salary of $20,000, we start the person at $20,000. Instead of saying a commission has issued a report criticizing the governor, we say the commission criticized the governor in a report. We delete the idea of issuing; if a report does some criticizing, we assume the act of issuing. Use verbs wisely, vigorously.

We have one more level of editing. This one inflicts its greatest suffering on people who edit their own stuff. Let's call it the Wholesale Deletion Phobia. We're afraid to make big cuts, afraid to eliminate long passages. More of us should practice more wholesale deletion. We need it on those paragraphs—sections, even—that do little more than rephrase information already presented. You know the problem. You have written a paragraph and, later, said substantially the same thing in another paragraph. You don't want to cut it, even if you recognize the repetition, for that would mean you had written the paragraph for nothing; you would have wasted your time. Well, to avoid that, I have this advice: Don't write one of those paragraphs.

One other thought: Maybe you haven't really wasted your time if you cut out some of your own goodies. Maybe the time you spend getting your material into better shape for your readers will help you get your message, your news, across more clearly and quicker. Maybe if you develop copy editor's mentality, you can do that every time you read over what you and the staff have written.

## Wanted: Editors

If you have a great interest in getting rich, you can start by figuring out a way to get more copy editors for newspapers. The demand grows daily. Even at weekly newspapers.

Why is that?

Students, the people I work with most, view copy editing as glamorless, joyless, unrewarding drudgery. Others share that view. Let's look.

Copy editors seldom get a great deal of recognition. Reporters forget the times editors have prevented costly errors; they remember butchery forever. Bosses seldom lavish attention on the copy desk; they expect perfection. The desk gets noticed when an editor fails to catch a reporter's mistake. That is, the copy editor is most likely to be visible when he or she allows an error to show up in print.

Great saves are invisible. Copy editors have to clean up all the grammar, keep us out of libel courts, correct the misspelled names and be alert enough to delete mistakes caused by haste. They do all that and write a selling headline in a couple of minutes. It's expected.

People outside the office have no idea of what copy editors do. A newspaper tour guide, taking a group past the desk, once said, "Those are copy editors. They fix things." The visitors were satisfied.

After the lack of recognition, we have to worry about working conditions. Editors do get to stay inside, out of the weather. You could look at that another way. They are confined. They see no new faces. They go to no exotic places. They have no expense accounts. They never move in new circles. They don't watch history being made; they just put it together. No excitement there.

Desk hours are moderately long, though not killing. Desk denizens work odder hours—sometimes past midnight or before 6 a.m., depending on publication times. Odd hours take a toll on families.

Pressure bears more heavily on desk people than on most others. When they miss deadlines, the delay has a direct effect of making the newspaper come out late. Often, they have to try to make up time lost by others in getting the copy to the desk. They cannot work ahead; they must wait for copy, no matter how late it arrives.

We add frustration to all the above—frustration at being unable to give every story the polishing a word lover would like to give.

So, how do we turn all this around?

As a publisher, I would start with a boost in recognition. Offer bonuses to the desk for good work. Headlines are the easiest to praise. Kind words should go on the bulletin board with regularity. The copy chief might call attention to interesting saves—in which an error is spotted and deleted before publication. These could be posted in the newsroom. The managing editor might take one subeditor at a time or the whole desk staff out for lunch. A newspaper with assigned parking spaces could raise the priority for the desk.

What else can you do? Try rotation. Let every editor work a week or two on a beat, if he or she wants to. Get every reporter to work on the desk for one or two weeks a year, regardless of preferences. Let them see how problems appear from the other side.

Ease more reporters into occasional desk work. Some may find they like it. You may find potential editor timber. The experience will help everyone involved.

Reduce the number of hours editors work. Really. Sure, I know I'm spending someone else's money. But copy editors work too hard at most places. They often do three jobs; they edit, read proof, and then give typesetting commands to computerized machines. Spend some of the savings on more people and fewer hours.

Boost the pay. Newspapers typically pay desk people more than reporters, partly because of the nature of the work and partly to lure more people. The *Baltimore Sun* pays a copy editor $30 a week more than a reporter in the basic contract, or it did when I last checked. That isn't out of line. Newspapers editors have extra work, what with electronic typesetting now almost universal. Although they do three jobs, they get paid for one.

No, they should not get triple pay. But they ought to get more than they do, and we ought to have more people doing this interesting, challenging, sometimes killing work. It's not a bad way to make a living.

# Ten Timely Tips: Things an Editor Should Know—and Do

My favorite editing book[1] has a section called "Ten Timely Tips." (The book's author is fond of such highly imaginative subheads.)

These tips, though second nature to many of you, contain in-

---

1. *Editing in the Electronic Era.* I wrote this marvelous book myself, which may influence my opinion of it.

junctions that all young editors ought to learn and all old editors ought to remember. I use one or more just about every day.

Let's look at the list:

1. Mumble.
2. Add it up.
3. Verify or duck.
4. Ask the old-timers.
5. Compress.
6. Chop fearlessly.
7. Do the work only once.
8. Be alert for repetition.
9. Avoid procrastination.
10. Recheck.

These helped me catch two errors in the last newspaper I read before starting this piece.

The first tip, "Mumble," is less an encouragement for imperfect diction than a reminder to you to get facts fixed in your mind as you read, rather than just skimming. When you meet a name in a news story, mumble it to yourself. Get it fixed. I did that on a guy named Neilson. I nailed that in my mind. Then, in the third paragraph, when he was referred to as Neilsen, I figured something was wrong. So I went through the story and found that the name was spelled with two *e*'s the rest of the way.

Not five minutes later I ran into a story telling about a car race in which the winner did 719 laps at 114 mph and covered 1,760.96 miles. The next paragraph said that broke a record on the 3.84-mile track. The old record was 715 laps, or 2,724.60 miles.

You have enough information to see the error, in this case a simple typo. We got tipped off by the 1,000-mile difference, or at least we should have. But not all typos have an accompanying figure to get them exposed. How many typos go uncaught because we don't add up (or multiply) the figures? Too many to count. So Tip 2 helped us here.

I realize that copy editors do not always have idle time available to play with their calculators. (Any publisher too stingy to buy a calculator for the copy chief deserves to have math mistakes in the newspaper.)

I am sort of partial to No. 3, "Verify or duck," as one of the better tips. The tip means that if you spot some questionable material but can't check it out before deadline, you ought to write around it. Duck it. Dodge it.

If you firmly believe Frank Knox was FDR's secretary of the Army but the story says secretary of the Navy, just say he was in the Cabinet. Your first goal, easily the better idea, is to check it. Duck the facts only if you cannot check them. You give your readers less information than you would like, but you don't give wrong information.

I once worked on a newspaper that had some youngsters from out of state on the copy desk. Most of them did a fine job. However, now and then they had questions. They made use of Tip 4 by asking an old-timer questions like these: Where's Panola County? Who shares the Permanent University Fund? Didn't Sissy Farenthold run for governor?

Old hands know the answers and don't mind sharing their wisdom. Veterans also don't mind answering style questions, although a questioner can run that practice into the ground in a hurry if he or she shows no signs of trying to learn the book.

Now we'll hit No. 5, "Compress." Copy editors almost always delete material. They take out superfluous wording. They try to retain all the meaning in fewer words. They don't write in shorthand. They compress by making every word carry a full share of the freight. Example:

> The scientist said the boom was either locked in position or so close that the difference is unimportant.

Compressed:

> The scientist said the boom was firmly in place.

Another example:

> A workshop was held Thursday night at which the directors discussed several people being considered for the job.

Compressed:

> Directors discussed candidates for the job at a workshop Thursday night.

You don't have to say the workshop was held. If something happened there, surely it was held.

You can compress most material. Just make sure you don't squeeze the life out of it.

We continue with the 10 timely tips.

No. 6: "Chop fearlessly." Most of us have no trouble chopping wire copy. In the old days, we would hold it up and cut it off where it hit the floor. Now we do the same thing electronically, although I hope most of us take a little more care than we did in those days of butchery.

At any rate, a copy editor must realize that he or she will go home knowing more about the news than most readers do. We have to cut some good material out of many stories. Accept that. Understand a story. Then cut it without looking back. If you truly understand a story, you are unlikely to butcher it.

Most of us find that chopping our own copy is a bit more difficult. We figure that if we go to the trouble of writing something, it must be good. So we hesitate to throw it out. That habit contributes to more poor writing than most other habits do. You will never approach perfection until you can cut the fat out of your own material.

No. 7: "Do the work only once." That means you need to make big cuts first, rather than doing a lot of meticulous editing on a paragraph before you kill the whole paragraph anyway.

No. 8: "Be alert for repetition." Repetition can come in the form of a false lead or an elegant variation later in a story. You may use the term *throwaway lead*. You recognize it as the first paragraph of the following:

> James Jones may be the first person ever robbed by a basketball team.
>
> Five tall young men marched into his delicatessen Monday night and took $1,500 from Jones and six customers.

Actually, that's not a horrible lead if Jones brings up the basketball angle himself. (He may have thought they were going to slam-dunk him.) However, we want to be careful about forcing the idea into the story. Anyway, the first sentence can be discarded with no loss, if we give Jones a first name in the second paragraph.

That part about elegant variation includes some variation not so elegant. Some of us just get in a hurry and keep writing while our mental engine is idling. We keep putting things on paper, but we aren't thinking new thoughts. Be careful. Don't let yourself or your reporters repeat information in new form.

No. 9: "Avoid procrastination." Oh, but I wish I could follow my own advice all the time. The habit would come in handy at those times I see something in a story and tell myself I must check it out. In a minute. And then I forget it. Or maybe I think of a truly brilliant way to say something (OK, a *good* way to say it), but I don't want to pause to write it down. Then I forget that I was going to change anything or at least I forget forever the exact wording. Had I not put it off, I would have made the world a better place.

No. 10: "Recheck." Good copy editors tend to have a mixture of humility and arrogance in their makeup. Their arrogance—maybe it's confidence—arises from their work. They have to improve things all the time. They must feel sure of themselves. Their humility comes from the realization that they have imperfections. An editor who knows everything and thinks he or she is incapable of error is in trouble.

Maybe we can skip the philosophy. Maybe we can just say that every person who strokes a keyboard for a living must learn to go back over all copy.

That part is absolutely no fun. You have edited your stuff, and you know it's perfect. You're in a hurry. Why look at it one more time? Simple. Although all of us think we read proof as we edit, our minds play tricks and we do peculiar things. Extra letters. Extra spaces. Missing words. We have plenty of errors without encouraging more by hurrying.

That's it. I will quit here and read back over this. Right now.

# Statistics

This sentence should bother you: *The average wage for workers at the plant was about $11 to $12 an hour.*

Get rid of the double approximation. We need nothing more than the word *about.* Say the average was about $11 an hour. That indicates we do not have the precise figure, just something in the neighborhood. You could go the other way and say workers average $11 to $12 an hour. That also indicates inexactness. Go either way, but do not fire both barrels of approximation. One will do.

Let's give this poor sentence some more scrutiny and then move on to today's main sermon. Follow the copy editor's basic rule of math: Every figure needs another figure.

Actually, that statement runs a little strong, because some figures get along by themselves. But many need help if we are to understand them.

You know averages come in three denominations: mean, median and mode. Most of the time we have the mean in mind when we refer to average. You get the mean in wages, for example, by adding up all the wages and dividing by the number on the payroll. That's what we have here, with $11 to $12 an hour. But we do not know how many workers we are talking about, nor how the wages range.

Sometimes a simple average leads us down the wrong path. Sometimes we would have a better picture if we had the mode, the most common wage figure. For example, if you have nine persons making $5 an hour and one making $65, they average $11 an hour. But to say the average wage was $11 an hour would be to mislead every reader; 90 percent of the people make less than half that. We're better off saying: *The typical employee gets $5 an hour.*

Most of the time your income figures will show more variety—say, some at $4, some at $5 or $10 or $12, and so on. In such a case, the *median* can improve understanding. Everyone knows about highway medians. Statistical medians are sort of the same. The median is the halfway figure: Half our people make less than a certain amount an hour and half make more. If we know that kind of average, we know something about the company.

Let's look at some cases of a figure needing another. When you get down to it, this just means you need to supply perspective and a concrete example for abstractions. You do the concreteness trick regularly with something like a tax story. The story tells us about an increase in rates, possibly using terms like *mill* and *ad valorem.* You must tie these to something readers can understand, such as the amount of increase on a $100,000 house. You could use $50,000, but $100,000 is easier on people doing math. The requirements change a little for income tax figures that readers can relate to. You probably will not list all choices, from a $10,000 income in a family of six to a $200,000 income in a two-yuppie household. But you need to give a majority of readers some idea of how the change will affect them. You have a lot more readers making $30,000 than $200,000, so you must accommodate them. Use meaningful figures, something close to what your readers earn.

How about perspective? Some writers almost go out of their way to be vague in statistics stories. For instance, a note that retail sales increased 10 percent in a month has no meaning by itself. Retail sales in December always outpace those of November by more than 10 percent. You have to compare like with like, meaning this December with last December. You know that, because it's so obvious at Christmastime. It's less obvious at other times and in other kinds of statistics. But being less obvious does not make perspective less important. Provide it.

I saw a good example in the *Colorado Springs Gazette-Telegraph.* The story noted that 66 of 81 police officers at an association meeting had voted "no confidence" in their chief. Then the story told us the department has nearly 400 officers. That might indicate lack of interest. But then came a quote that most association meetings drew only a dozen officers. So we get some idea of interest and feeling.

Sometimes, we distort the picture severely by not having raw figures to go with percentages. You might be surprised to know that one year 33 percent of the coeds at Johns Hopkins University married faculty members. You would be less surprised if you knew that the school had only three female students that year, the first year that women were allowed to enroll.

I got that from Darrell Huff's *How to Lie With Statistics,* a splendid little book available in many college bookstores (no, I do not know the percentage) or from the publisher, W.W. Norton & Co. of New York.

Huff gives good examples of the abuse of statistics. In one, the Navy notes that only nine sailors per thousand die in wartime, whereas the death rate for people in New York is 16 per thousand. That means it's safer to be a sailor in war than a resident of New York. Wrong. You have to take a physical exam to get into the Navy. You don't even need a mental exam to get into New York. The New York death figure includes everyone, not just healthy people 17 to 40 years old.

That gets us to the post hoc fallacy: If *B* follows *A,* then *A* causes *B.* This lies at the base of superstition. Athletes eat this up. They have more rituals than the College of Cardinals. Some coaches wear the same necktie to every game. I'm sure that if a coach accidentally tied his shoelaces in a knot before a game and his team scored an upset, he would forever after go around with knotted laces. True story: My high school basketball coach didn't get the uniforms washed after a season-opening loss, and we won the next game. So he skipped the washer for the game after that, too. We won again. That team won 26 straight games, in unwashed uniforms. I do not recall whether we were ranked in the state, but we were rank.

# Five Questions for Users of Statistics

Some more on Darrell Huff and *How to Lie With Statistics.* Huff offers five questions that journalists might ask when examining statistics. Actually, he doesn't mention journalists, but reporters and editors need the advice even more than other people. The questions:

1. Who says so?
2. How does he know?
3. What's missing?

4.  Did someone change the subject?
5.  Does it make sense?

Although neither Huff nor I would want to breed a race of cynics, journalists do need to note whether someone has something to gain by offering statistics. For example, look at polls financed by political candidates. You need all the raw data you can get if you want to avoid being hoodwinked. It's not that candidates are evil; they just like to put the best face on every number.

You will sometimes get a peculiar answer when you ask how someone knows something offered as a fact. In the first place, polltakers know only what people tell them, not necessarily what's true. Ask students their grade point averages. You will not get low estimates. Most students round things off. Thus a 2.377 is rounded to "just under 3.0." Also, biased samples can render figures meaningless. A question about drinking, asked outside a bar just after midnight Saturday, will produce answers different from the same question asked outside a church 12 hours later.

We covered the third question earlier, noting that raw figures sometimes tell a lot more than percentages, for example. Here's one to watch for: Check the highway fatality reports on the next holiday. The nation will have, say, 600 fatalities on the long weekend. To be meaningful, that story must tell us how many fatalities a normal weekend and Monday would include. I do not mean to belittle 600 deaths, but people needn't do any extra teeth-gnashing if the rate is somewhere near normal.

As for changing the subject, you have to be ready. It happens all the time. For example, you may see some reference to prison expenditures amounting to $150 a day per inmate. Then comes a sentence saying these people could get a good room in the Waldorf-Astoria for less. The subject changed: The hotel reference omits the cost of guards, food, uniforms and so on.

I like No. 5 best. Does it make sense? We see a lot of refined nonsense in the world of statistics. Much involves interpolation, making estimates based on trends. The number of videocassette recorders doubled between 1983 and 1985 and doubled again by 1987. Therefore, by the turn of the century we will have so many VCRs that you will have to kick them out of the way to get into your house. Does that make sense? This challenging question would have kept the Navy from making that statement (mentioned a minute ago) about it being safer to be a sailor in wartime than a civilian in New York. That doesn't make sense, and a questioner should have noticed that New York outpaces the Navy in people being about ready to die from natural causes.

Let me return to No. 2 with a reference to another book, the *Handbook of Reporting Methods,* by Cleveland Wilhoit and Maxwell McCombs. (McCombs works where I do, if that makes any difference to you.) They offer advice to people who report on polls. In order to present an honest picture, they suggest, you need answers to the following questions:

Who sponsored the poll?

Who was interviewed? Homeowners? Voters? People passing on the street? Whites only?

How were subjects chosen? (In a random poll, everyone has an even chance of being interviewed. You can limit the universe, picking no one but voters, for example, but everyone in the universe must have an equal opportunity to give an opinion.)

How many people were interviewed? (Ten would be too few, generally. You would not need 10,000. Properly chosen, a sample of 1,500 would handle almost any polling requirement for reliability. Good pollsters will not object to this question.)

What is the sampling error? (Statisticians give you a plus-or-minus number called sampling error. It means that half the time your results should fall within this range. If an IQ test has a tolerance of plus or minus 3, that means a person who scored 101 would score between 98 and 104 half the time if retested. The person could score more, or less, the other times. The bigger the sampling error, the less reliable the figures.)

Who did the interviewing, and how and when? (You need to know whether you are dealing with phone calls or personal interviews. Was the interviewing done by professionals or campaign volunteers? How old are the data? One of the last world-class polling errors occurred in 1948. Polltakers quit work two weeks before the election, when Harry Truman was considered hopelessly behind in his race with Thomas Dewey. You probably do not remember President Dewey.)

What were the questions? (As a reporter, you need the questions so you can see what inferences are being drawn. People can give one answer if asked which candidate they consider the best qualified and quite another answer if asked for whom they would vote if the election were held today. I have voted for a lot of people who were not as well qualified as others, though I did not always discover that until they were in office.)

Finally, you should ask how the data were tabulated and analyzed. For example, a poll asking about political candidates will be more reliable if polltakers filter out people who aren't likely to vote than if everyone questioned is included in the math.

Let me close with a paraphrase from Wilhoit and McCombs: If you check the polling and are satisfied it's legitimate, you do not have to tell readers every tiny detail. But you have to provide enough for them to evaluate the results. Answers to most of these questions can be slipped into the story unobtrusively, or they can be run as a sidebar. They need to be somewhere readers can find them. That is simply responsible journalism.

# A Statistical Quiz

You will be offered 10 sentences with statistical problems. Your job will be to see how the logic fails to match up with the figures. Not all are wrong; some are just meaningless.

1. The state sureties board allowed brokers to raise their deposit requirements by 5 percent Tuesday, from 20 percent to 25 percent of the value of a stock.
2. Last year, sharks attacked nearly 12 times as many male swimmers as females off U.S. beaches. Some researchers believe one of the sexes has a slightly different odor that causes sharks to either avoid or attack persons of that sex.
3. The doctor said 66-69 percent of his patients who take birth control pills suffer discomfort from contact lenses.
4. Eleven nations have improved their infant mortality rates more than the United States since 1960, indicating a decline in health care in this country.
5. Among 95 percent of the couples seeking divorce, one or both partners do not attend church regularly, the vicar said in concluding that churchgoers stay married.
6. Jones said the new tempering process, involving a cold-water dip, made the steel three times harder.
7. Soopa bread contains only three-fourths as many calories per slice as the best-selling breads.
8. The provost noted that one-third of the women who entered the university's first class had married faculty members.
9. In Illinois, the average boy starts shaving at age 16.537.

   10. Executives of the company own an average of 600 shares
of stock.

   Now let's look at those examples.
   1. That deposit went up five percentage points, but the increase, from 20 to 25, was 25 percent.
   2. For this to make sense, we must know more. If sharks do
not attack within 100 yards of shore, let's say, and if 12 times as many
males as females go 100 yards offshore, the rate is the same for people
susceptible to shark attack. On the other hand, if 12 times as many
women as men go 100 yards out, the sharks' preference for males is
much more pronounced.
   3. This has no significance if 66-69 percent of those who do
not take the pill also suffer discomfort. If only 10 percent of the non-
users have pain, we're onto something.
   4. Where did we start? If a country has a low rate, it will
show little progress. A country with a high rate could cut it in half and
still have problems. But it would have made great statistical gains.
Raw figures would help us understand this better.
   5. We need a figure on church attendance for people who do
not get divorces. We cannot dispute the vicar's figures, but they tell us
nothing by themselves.
   6. Harder than what? Is it harder than all steel tempered the
old-fashioned way? Is it harder than it would be if not tempered at all?
People give us fuzzy figures like this all the time. Journalists must get
rid of the fuzziness.
   7. Sounds impressive? Let's make sure we are all singing off
the same page. How big is a slice? If Soopa's slices are half as thick as
other bread slices, it will probably have only half the calories automatically. Watch out for this basic form of dishonesty. Others that come to
mind: how far a car will travel on a tank of gasoline, how long it takes
to read a book. Look for more.
   8. This one appeared in the section "Statistics" in this chapter. The opening class had three females. One wed a prof. That hardly
establishes a trend.
   9. How in the world do we know this about shavers? Isn't
that figure too precise? It appears to pinpoint the first encounter to the
day, almost to the morning or afternoon. Besides, aren't kids likely to
lie a little about when they passed this early test of manhood? Sure.
For this one, we should ask some of the five questions listed earlier,
including "Does it make sense?"

10. A median might be more helpful in our understanding of stock ownership. Raw figures would be nice. If we learned that one fellow owned 5,100 shares and nine owned 100 each, we would see that this average of 600 shares gave us a false picture.

People throw false pictures at us all the time. Editors and reporters have to be alert to keep from passing bad information on to readers. Some people mislead us on purpose; some do it out of ignorance. Makes no difference. Our job is to write precisely, and to do that we have to understand a little about the ways people manipulate numbers.

# 8

# Newspaper Thoughts

A look in the mirror • A goal or two or nine • Planning •
Strategy for success • Questions from readers •
Localization I: stealing ideas • Localization II: bringing
stories home • Localization III: bringing the world to town

## A Look in the Mirror

Newspaper chains, or groups, like to have reports from outposts in their far-flung empires. Newspaper people out there do not
like to write reports. Groups probably need fewer reports, and editors
probably need to do more.

Even editors who do not have to report to someone in a higher
position ought to make some formal assessment with regularity. I will
settle for an annual summation, as long as it's thorough.

We are not dealing with the profit-and-loss statement here. I
mean we ought to take time, at least once a year, to set down our goals
and count our successes and failures.

The inspiration for this thought comes from Roy Smith,
publisher of the *Colorado Springs Gazette-Telegraph*. Mr. Smith, a gra-
cious soul, let me look at a 12-page accounting of his newsroom's performance for a year. Interesting.

He and his staff assessed every part of the paper. The assessment ran from typography, including logos, folios, nameplate and
cutlines type, to sentence length. It dealt with the choice of syndicated
columnists. It talked of a new rule requiring at least two reads on the
copy desk for every story.

I thought beer and scenery were the best things found in Colorado, but this idea may be of more value.

If I were an editor, I would make a checklist covering the whole paper. I might even break that down into times – do this the first month and that the second month and that other the third. Then at the end of the year, we could see what else we had to do.

Let me cite a few items worth examination and possible treatment in your annual assessment:

Nameplate. Do you have a long notice, like *Price 25 cents per copy,* or do you just use a sensible *25¢*? The former wastes words. People can assume that *25¢* relates to price. Is your nameplate clean and the type legible? Does it make some kind of statement about the paper?

Cutlines. How do you set them? How are the size, face, margins, gap between columns, and credit line done?

Headlines. Check sizes, vertical and horizontal spacing, and darkness, not to mention quality of content.

Index. Readable? Necessary?

Standing headlines, column headings.

Jumps. Number, placement, jump lines, jump head style.

Briefs. Number, length (some aren't brief briefs) and location.

Editorial page. Has it been changed this century? Why do we run the columnists we run? Habit?

Color. Is it truly more expensive than we can afford?

Feedback. Do reporters get praise and criticism? Does the copy desk get the same? Ever praise a photographer? (This does not apply if you are the photographer.)

Promotion. Do staffers know how they get promoted? Do they know how their work is assessed? Do they feel boxed in? Do they have a chance to make as much contribution to the paper as they can? Do you want them to grow? Do you stretch them?

Sports. Just what do we cover? Could we cover it better? How? Do sports pages look like sports pages, full of life and vigor?

Calendar. Do we carry a good list of events in the community?

Type. Have we looked at our body type and decided it's the best we can have?

Content. Do we show enterprise, or do we just react to events? How far ahead do we plan? Do we ever get out a ruler and see just how much wire news we run? How much local? How much international? Do we know how many Page One local stories we ran last month? Do we care?

Length. How often do we run padded stories – stories so long no one would read them? Do our people rewrite their own work to shorten it, or do they just cut something?

Packaging. Do we think about photography only after a reporter has come back with the story? Do we consider graphs and charts and maps?

As I say, the *Gazette* list runs 12 pages. We may not want to make such a thorough examination of our own papers, but we should find some sort of look worthwhile.

# A Goal or Two or Nine

A group of newspeople brought together by the *New York Times* has compiled a document on the things newspapers ought to do. Some of the material makes sense to me. So let's look at it.

You will notice some overlap in these items. We have to pursue the news a little more aggressively, and most of these points make that statement in one way or another; hence the overlap.

The document says newspapers should provide these things:

1. Must reading for people with high socioeconomic status and low news interest
2. Local ties
3. A frame of reference
4. Grist for conversation
5. A quick-read capability
6. Utility
7. Multiple points of entry to stories
8. News stories whose tone matches the content
9. Broad-based feature coverage, carefully tailored to local interests

I hate to start with a sentence that contains a word as fancy as *socioeconomic,* but that has to do with important items. It refers to news about business, politics, the economy, the future . . . all kinds of interesting things. Indeed, it would not take much of a stretch for us to cover the bulk of serious news with this point, from Iran to a flood.

Most of what we cannot cover with No. 1 we can get with No. 2. Localization "can be defined in terms of civic activities, employers, institutions, geography, leisure and even people," the report said. This would include things all people have an interest in, from hospital research in New Orleans to a report on Mexico for areas along the border. It would cover leisure time, from opera to gardening, from wrestling to bicycling. It would cover familiarity of place, perhaps a Know Your Heritage feature every week (a series on history, houses, neighborhoods, parks, general scenes). The *Orange County Register* in Santa Ana, Calif., has a feature called Freeze Frame. It puts a new photo of some site next to an old picture of the same place. The *Victor Valley Daily Press,* also from California, has a weekly feature called Just a Tankful Away. It tells readers what they can find within driving distance for a weekend.

We can say more about this No. 2. We could do religion stories, including some that deal with moral issues instead of just a list of church doings. And we could get reader participation, from guest columns to man-on-the-street interviews. We could run stories on the 10 best (or worst) jobs in town. Get ministers to recall their best sermons. Get the high school coaches to recall their 10 best victories or 10 most memorable losses. The field is limitless.

In No. 3 we deal with a frame of reference. Newspapers must provide familiarity and consistency to help readers understand the news. We have to give people a starting point for their discussions.

No. 4, grist for conversation, calls for an abundance of tidbits, serious gee-whiz-Martha stories, crime and other things people talk about. People use us for their information, and we need to be sure they have reason to stay with us. You know you have written a clear story if you hear two people discussing it—with some understanding. (Gee-whiz-Martha story: A husband, reading the newspaper at the breakfast table, says to his wife: "Gee whiz, Martha, here's a great story.")

Our quick-read capability, No. 5, can make a contribution. We can provide capsule treatments, indexes, charts and summaries that give people a modest understanding of a story at one glance. Most people do not read complete stories anyway, and we have to cater to them. This does not mean we must all become *USA Today* in our shallowness. It means we have to offer something for people who wade in only up to their ankles as well as for those who plunge in headfirst.

Certainly we have to have something of utility, as noted in No. 6. That is, we must give readers movie and TV listings, classified ads, meaningful weather reports (detailing effects on travel, clothing, sports and so on). We must tell about jobs, self-help, health, religion, diet, hobbies—in a word, consumerism. We have to offer what one newsman referred to as the "triumph of the useful over the merely interesting."

I probably should have put No. 7, about multiple points of entry, back there with the bit on quick reading. But you must realize that people get hooked on a story a number of ways. A headline will usually do it. A photograph can be better, if strong enough. Charts and graphs help as stoppers, and their information can pull a reader into the story.

Some newspapers never really know their audiences, and therefore they have trouble matching the tone to the content, as No. 8 suggests. That is, they do not know what the content means to different groups. An urban newspaper that does not consider itself the main source of news might adopt a friendly tone, with a lot of direct address. The *New York Times,* on the other hand, takes a more formal approach, and its tone matches its content. In some cases, you would target the tone to a specific group of people. The young might get something sassy or irreverent. You also establish tone through graphics. You can shed the image of an old-fashioned, stuffy newspaper and offer a modern face.

And we end with No. 9, an appeal for broad-based feature coverage. Lifestyle sections do not have as strong an appeal to women who have a low news interest as sports have to men with a low interest level. We have to offer material, from wine to fitness, from books to household hints, to be sure we offer these people something they want and need.

# Planning

If I were called upon to improve the quality of my newspaper, I would draw up a plan.

That thought no doubt makes sense to most newspaper editors, but not enough of them ever put their views down on paper; those plans live only in an editor's brain. Most of us want to put out better newspapers or, as in my case, see better newspapers put out. But we don't organize our thoughts. We do the work a day at a time, crisis to crisis. A written plan would help.

I'll offer some thoughts on the subject. My editor-friends can enjoy a laugh, perhaps, because they sit closer to reality than I do. But maybe I will get close enough to some point to stimulate some thoughts in newsrooms.

First off, you have to decide what you want the newspaper to be and what makes a good newspaper. You must make money, of course, but you surely go beyond that. You want to tell the people of your city about things that affect them. You want to give them information they can use to make their lives more pleasant today and tomorrow. You want to help them govern themselves. You want to make a contribution to the city's thinking, the way people look at their civic problems. You might even want to tell people how to act, though you're probably doomed to frustration if you really want to run things. About the best you can do is get people to talk about the things you want talked about. (Academicians call this agenda-setting.)

From here you have to see what kind of reporter strength you have. Do you cover everything? Do you cover it well? Do your reporters have time to look at records and discuss governmental business with the people involved? Or does a reporter have to move to something else after covering the council meeting? Does this lack of time cause the reporter to leave council statements unquestioned or unverified?

At some point, finances enter the picture. You have to decide whether you need another reporter more than a sun room or a new car. (For what it's worth, few dead people are remembered for sun rooms or the kind of car they drove. Now and then, of course, someone — Hearst and Vanderbilt come to mind — erects a dwelling that lives after him. Some of the Tut boys from Egypt managed it, too. But I digress.) News coverage ought to be a specific part of any plan for improvement. The editor should write down the ideal coverage arrangement and see how close he or she can come to it.

An editor must also have a plan for improving the quality of writing, editing, photography and layout. This job does not get done overnight.

You also have to decide how much editorial leadership you will provide. I cannot discuss this for an individual, for each city is different. I only hope editors do not let fear turn them away from taking a position. An editor who gets lumps on his head can be forgiven if he decides not to take another shot at the lumper. But an editor who shuns a scrap without knowing he will be opposed is to be pitied.

Now some specifics. A publisher who does not know what employees think is hunting for treasure with half a map. A sensible boss will ask employees how they could do their work better. I'm not thinking about an anonymous suggestion box. I mean regular, sit-down conferences. I don't mean an editor should be calling people into the office; I'm talking about going to the composing room or the newsroom. If people understand that an improvement in the quality of their section, and certainly of their own work, means they get more money, they will take an interest.

The task of improving writing and editing boils down to self-examination — some editors do all the writing, editing, photography and layout themselves. Others, those with newsroom help, need to start by letting employees know the boss wants improvement. If it is not abundantly clear that improvements in skills will be rewarded, the employee has little incentive to go all out on getting better. Money alone won't do the trick; some recognition has to come into play somewhere. You know these other forms of encouragement, from choice of contest entries to bulletin board comments, from bylines to a plain statement, made aloud, that a worker has done a good job.

I like to discuss self-improvement, because I believe the observant beginner can improve even if an editor has no time to help. Other forms of help are available, from news clinics to books and columns. Editors need to make sure the staff has books available. Books alone will not teach someone to write better. However, they indicate an interest in writing, and they contribute to that interest; it feeds on itself. The person who gets interested in writing is more likely than others to improve his or her ability.

An editor bent on improving the newspaper must also arrange for feedback from the community. Feedback from close friends on the golf course generally fails to qualify here. You need to know what your subscribers think. You have to ask them. You ask them with house ads inviting their views. You ask them with a meeting. You can have coffee and cake for a hundred people—chosen numerically from your subscription list or chosen some other way to take care of non-subscribers. Or you can have a fish fry, a barbecue, a sit-down dinner. Your stamina and your pocketbook govern the kind of gathering you have. Just remember to tell the people they are going to get a chance to tell you how to run the newspaper.

I have already mentioned the need for community involvement. You may get some suggestions when you have your meeting with your readers. More likely, the level of your involvement will be reflected in favorable comments at the meeting.

Community involvement comes under the heading of good public relations, and many editors aren't interested in that subject. A pity. If you can sponsor a softball home-run contest or a 10-K run or a bicycle ride, you get your name in front of the people in a positive way. You remind them you are there as a friend. If you get people to contribute stories or ideas, you are ahead. If you get people to help you make predictions—about elections, about the next year, about football games—you are ahead. If you get people to come into the office because they consider it a friendly place and they want to help you, you are ahead.

And ahead is where I would like to be if I were an editor.

# Strategy for Success

"All strategic plans have two elements: 1) setting goals, and 2) developing methods of achieving the goals."

The quotation comes from a booklet by the Newspaper Advertising Bureau. The booklet, entitled *Readers: How to Gain and Retain Them,* was sent to all newspapers. You ought to look at it.

It examines newspaper problems in this time of declining readership, and it offers some thoughts on changing the picture. Burl Osborne of the *Dallas Morning News* wrote much of it, as you can see from a section on building brand loyalty, a favorite Osborne theme. Although he edits a large newspaper, Osborne has some thoughts applicable to newspapers of all sizes, including weeklies.

*Readers* has something to say to managers and others. It reminds us that the production of newspaper requires teamwork. It outlines the big picture. It gets down to detail. And it lets you—no, requires you—to adapt its wisdom to your own circumstances.

I like the emphasis on content, but the strategy sections will help some people more. A quote: "The single most important aspect of strategic planning is getting all your people moving in the same direction. That perforce means they must participate in the selection of goals—or at the very least know what the goals are."

*Readers* proceeds from there through a look at the elements of planning, especially that need for getting all players oriented toward clearly defined goals. (You do have your goals on paper, don't you?) It runs through competitive strategy, including a look at customers; you have to know your target audience, your area and of course yourself. A week spent on a hard look at the paper—examining weaknesses, strengths, gaps—could produce dividends for most editors.

Content gets full coverage, for the ad bureau recognizes the contribution of news. *Readers* has much to say about the value of a good reputation and about the difficulty of erasing a bad reputation.

Editorials and columns get examined, too. Moreover, the booklet notes that readers must be brought into the process through letters, guest columns, panels and other things you think up.

"Newspapers that achieve and retain competitive advantage with readers will never, ever finish improving themselves," the booklet says. "Innovation is a continuous process. The most successful innovation usually is not achieved by waking up one day and discovering a breakthrough. It is more often finding ways, one at a time, to do a better job at what already is being done."

*Readers* also goes through the distribution system, including sales, promotion, and circulation pricing and strategy. It also has a section about starting a readership committee.

You will like the *Readers* approach, which includes a quiz after each segment. The booklet gives you only *yes* and *no* as choices for answers, but you are far more likely to answer with "Hey, that's a good idea" or "We ought to look into that." Much of it is directed at publishers. All is directed at managers. Most is helpful to editors.

You can get copies of the booklet by writing the Newspaper Advertising Bureau, Inc., 1180 Avenue of the Americas, New York, N.Y. 10036.

Now we close with some sample questions, from different sections:

> Do you know where the obits were today? Is that where they were yesterday (or last week, if you're a weekly)?
> Can a newcomer read your newspaper every day for a month and understand what your city is about?
> Have you explained the goals of the paper to the subordinates who must make them work?
> Has your paper produced a research report for your advertisers?
> Do you know the likely population of your market at the end of this century?
> Does your paper contain the basic information about your community in every issue—police news, obituaries, government, business, community events, entertainment, sports, and so on, plus a decent diet of national and world news?
> Has your total newsprint waste percentage decreased over the past six months?
> Have you written down the arguments that salespeople can use to overcome objections?
> Are new subscribers given a chance to critique the paper after their first month or so? Does someone read and act on the critiques?
> Do you know where your newspaper is, where it wants to go and how it wants to get there?

# Questions from Readers

The *Daily Star-Progress,* a community newspaper in La Habra/ Brea, Calif., sometimes runs a full-page ad answering the 15 most frequently asked questions of readers.

You will be able to steal this good idea right off the rack. I can give you the questions, but you have to supply your own answers. Comments after the questions are mine.

1. How can I buy a past issue of the newspaper? The newspaper should tell how, where, when, for how much and how far back past issues are available.

2. How can I order a print of a photo that ran in the newspaper, and can I get copies of pictures that were not used?

3. Where should I send my news release? We ought to run this information regularly, along with a note encouraging people to contribute.

4. How do I get an obituary published? The *Star-Progress* runs free obits but sells space under Death Notices for relatives to run whatever thoughts they want.

5. How does the newspaper handle letters to the editor? People need to be reminded of your need for letters and your requirements.

6. Where do I send my engagement or wedding announcement? The *Star-Progress* requires that you fill out a questionnaire.

7. Will someone from the newspaper speak to my group? I hope the answer is yes. Newspapers need all the exposure they can get.

8. How can I find out when an article was published? The answer to this one changes as we get more and more information into the computer.

9. Do you have special listings for non-profit activities? This newspaper runs free notices in the classifieds. It lists dog, cat and bird shows; car, plane, boat and recreational vehicle shows; scientific conventions; and reunions. The listing is done when space is available.

10. How can I place an ad in the newspaper? I suspect publishers would be happy to answer that question at some length. You ought to be surprised that it would make a list of often-asked questions. Its appearance on the list means we have some missionary work to do. Some of the heathen have not heard the word.

11. Can my family tour the newspaper? I hope so.

12. How can I subscribe to the newspaper? If No. 10 caught

your eye, this one should grab your throat. A lot of people don't know much about us.

13. How can I get permission to reprint an article from the paper? Tell readers how to go about this. Remind them to give you the date and page number of the article. Otherwise you may get a request to reprint "that article on city government you ran a year or so ago."

14. Can my class at school get copies of the newspaper? The *Star-Progress* sends 35 free copies to any classroom in its circulation area once each semester, but to only one room per school. Teachers or principals have to make the order, and the paper runs five days behind.

15. Does the newspaper donate to charities? When I saw this question, I figured the *Star-Progress* would find some slick way to tell charity collectors to stay away. Not so. The newspaper contributes "a set percentage of our net profit to charities who do not receive financial support from the government." And it adds: "It is our goal to return as much as possible to the community in which we serve."

That's not a bad way to end a house ad.

Or a book section.

# Localization I: Stealing Ideas

Let's talk about stealing.

Or at least about borrowing.

If you prefer a more genteel term, we'll call it localization. By any name, it deserves attention. It can help you improve your newspaper.

You already know that, of course. I'm just reminding you to do something you may have let slide.

Localization comes in at least two categories. In one, we do a little work within a story. In the other, we grab a story idea we see somewhere else and turn it into a local piece.

Example: We see a wire story telling about trouble with some kind of hospital procedure in some far-off city. Before we run it, we call the local hospital or hospitals and learn that the procedure was once used here but has been dropped. We localize with a paragraph to that effect.

Example: We see a wire story, or run across a story in the exchanges, saying farmers in some other state have tried a new system in which they do not plow up last year's fields but merely plant new seeds right in the stubble. We check into this and find that two farmers in our county are going to try this system and that the county agent has seen enough to make him a believer. So we develop a complete new story on what local people are doing.

That's localization.

Two reasons for localization come readily to mind (a way of saying you can probably think of more, but this is all I can offer at the moment).

First, it makes the news more personal for our readers. Reading about something that will take $100 out of your own bank account is infinitely more interesting than reading about some fellow who lost a million in the grain market in Chicago.

Second, you come up with much more thorough coverage of your area if you steal ideas. You get tips on stories that you simply might not find otherwise.

Fortunately, the practice of stealing need not be limited to metropolitan newspapers. Anyone can steal. But you have to work at it. You can't just wait for things to drop out of the sky. You have to cultivate your ability. You have to develop the habit of looking at stories with the intention of adapting them to your situation. You have to realize the value of theft – and then get after it.

You start with alertness. And you start there by training the person who handles the wire, or the exchanges, to be on the lookout for stories that could benefit from a little localizing. Or a lot of localizing. You make sure the wire editor and the city desk are on the same wave length. A sensitive wire editor will know when it's wise to hold off for a day on some story so a reporter can work up a local story on the same subject – assuming the story cannot be produced today. Usually, a wire story and a local sidebar (or the other way around) make a more interesting package on one day than they would if run on consecutive days. This refers to features, mainly; you don't delay important news stories.

That wire editor will also know enough about the community to recognize when a wire story needs a paragraph or a sentence – sometimes just a clause – about the local situation.

In addition, you get everyone on the staff to develop the habit of looking at all news stories from outside with an eye toward stealing the story idea or adapting it for local consumption. We need to have the habit of asking "Could that happen here? Is it happening here?" every time we see something of interest.

Seriously, I am talking about nothing more than habit. I mean only that people should look at news stories with an intention of localizing them.

Again, localization is a way to bring something closer to the reader. And you make money when you bring things closer to your readers.

We're dealing with money, folks. Isn't that as local as you can get?

# Localization II: Bringing Stories Home

Bill Steven, former editor of the *Houston Chronicle* and then the *Minneapolis Tribune,* retired and started doing a monthly piece for *Editorial Focus,* the newsletter of the communication company Harte-Hanks. He invariably offered words of wisdom.

I invariably stole from him.

One of his offerings lamented newspapers' failure to localize the story of the death of Ray Kroc, the McDonald's hamburger mogul. In Bill's words: "Apparently not a single paper made a single call to the local McDonald's manager."

Good point. Bill Steven had to do some digging to find out that Americans buy 12 million McDonald's hamburgers a day and that more than 25,000 people have graduated from the chain's Hamburger University. That group would probably include the local manager, who should have something to say about the passing of the company founder.

Kroc's autobiography, along with the wire stories, told about the man's rise from paper cup salesman to maker of 15-cent hamburgers to multimillionaire. The local McDonald's franchise made a contribution to that empire. McDonald's has made a lot of people well-to-do; some got rich on Kroc's formula of "quality, service, cleanliness and value." We could have told people of the effects a McDonald's has on a community.

Every town with a McDonald's restaurant — 6,000 spots in the United States — would have some interest. Every person who has ever eaten at McDonald's — you supply the number, and make it large — would have a firsthand connection.

So Harte-Hanks papers were not alone in letting this story slip through.

Did we have a rare lapse there? No. We do the same thing on a lot of other stories. We get into a hurry and don't check out all the angles. We don't make a true effort to look for potential local angles in stories.

All kinds of stories.

From all over.

When Chrysler announces a record profit, a great rebound from near disaster, we should find out how the local dealers feel. Such stories are obvious in business. How about religion? If someone writes a book saying some people murdered the pope, surely we can find someone in our town with a thought about that.

We look at an event occurring elsewhere and ask some basic questions: Could that happen here? Does anyone here have particular knowledge about such a situation? What local ramifications will that event have?

We see a picture of a bridge collapsed by a heavy truck. Any weak bridges in our county? We see a sagging street, undermined by a broken main. How are our water lines? Our sewer lines? Arsonists burn a school. Do our schools and government buildings have any safeguards against arson? (I leave to you the worry about planting an idea in some idiot's head. A story should not be worded so as to seem like a suggestion that arson would be a snap.)

This localization habit can be developed; you do not have to be born with it. To encourage it in yourself, simply make a decision. You can start with this approach: Go through the latest issue of your newspaper and see how many stories could have had a local angle. Do that regularly. Before long, you will find yourself looking for local angles in stories before they are printed.

You do not have to have a wire service to do this sort of thing. Weeklies can do it. Simply start thinking about stories you see in whatever dailies you read – or even the stories you see on the TV news.

You won't have time to develop a long local piece on everything you see. No one expects you to. But if you make one story a week blossom with some local freshness, you will have improved your newspaper and given your readers a bigger reward than they would have had.

# Localization III: Bringing the World to Town

The *Hattiesburg* (Miss.) *American* has given localization a new dimension.

You may be able to steal the idea.

The *American* ran a number of stories showing how events in the underdeveloped world had an impact on Hattiesburg. They made great reading, they attracted attention, and they had some influence on the citizens' views.

People saw, more clearly than before, that international trade involves hometown people. They learned that every billion dollars in trade means 25,000 jobs, including some in Mississippi. And that gets your attention.

The stories were run as part of a study done by the University of Southern Mississippi and the World Bank. The idea, a bank spokesman said, "was to prove that any American newspaper can, just by looking at its own community, report news about the Third World its subscribers will read."

University researchers found that readership ranged from 38 to 57 percent, an impressive figure. Anything near 50 percent is quite good.

John Hamilton of the World Bank wrote some of the stories. (I would have been happier had the stories all been staff products. But that is not to say I found the stories full of propaganda for the World Bank.) Staffers wrote others. An editorial tied them all together and wrapped things up.

The series, entitled "Main Street Mississippi and the Third World," had stories like these:

1. Conversations with farmers who sell to exporters or to brokers who get products into international trade. Using a single person as a typical farmer helps humanize the story. We learned about a farmer who keeps an eye on international events because those riots and wars and things affect his market.

2. The increasing number of Third World students who come to Hattiesburg to study at the university. They have an impact. They spend money. They learn. They go home.

3. Cultural differences and similarities. All of us would benefit from knowing a little more about our planetary neighbors. One story used soccer as a medium. Soccer is a universal sport; the ball is round in any language.

4. A look at immigrants. We all run into immigrants, from people in Chinese or Vietnamese restaurants to legal and illegal aliens from Mexico. One story looked at contributions other cultures made to the Mississippi milieu.

5. A talk with an American who works overseas. The newspaper interviewed a petrochemical engineer who visits many countries.

6. An examination of protectionism. One story told what import restrictions mean, using Mississippians in anecdotes. We got views from two sides.

7. Thoughts on religion. This story centered on missionaries supported by local people. It could have been followed by something on the cultural side – how religions differ.

8. Travel for everyone. One story involved talks with travel agents – what they see and where they send or take people. Every travel agent should be able to provide names of people who have been to exotic places, and those people should be able to provide some interesting insights about the places visited.

Hamilton, the bank's writer, spent a month in Hattiesburg to gather information. That gave the newspaper a bit of help you don't have. But you can still do some of the things the *American* did.

Basically, you're trying to find out what happens after a farmer takes a wagonload of cotton to a gin or grain to an elevator. That cotton or grain doesn't disappear. It goes somewhere, for use in clothing or feeding someone, indirectly or directly (as meat or grain).

You will have to spend a little time to get stories like these. But they will broaden the horizons of your readers, not to mention your staff. They may even improve citizenship – people will understand the world and their role in it a little more thoroughly. Who could complain about that?

A newspaper that localizes stories about international trade, that makes real people out of statistics from somewhere far off deserves some kind words. I'll bet the *American* got some kind words and some gratitude, too. It deserves both.

And so will you if you put out the effort.

# 9

# Headlines and Kin

Headlines and cutlines are vital • Writing Headlines • *The key word. Padding is fatal. Qualification and attribution. Punctuation. Feature headlines. Headlines: nix on esoteric lingo* • Writing Cutlines

## Headlines and Cutlines Are Vital

Newspaper people have the right idea, of course.

That is, they know people ought to spend an hour getting news from our product. Readers ought to go beyond headlines. They ought to read cutlines carefully. They ought to go through the lead to the meat of the story.

They don't.

Indeed, an interesting new piece of research indicates that headlines, cutlines and leads too often form barriers to readers. Readers don't cross those barriers; they turn to the TV or some other diversion.

Publisher John Ginn, writing in the Harte-Hanks *Editorial Focus,* tells about research done at his newspapers, the *Anderson Independent-Mail* of South Carolina. We need to listen.

His researchers, using groups of people brought in to discuss problems at length, found headlines, cutlines and leads to be the main sources of complaint. The top gripe about headlines: being misled. "Just give me the information in the headline and don't play games with me," one reader said.

This led Ginn, and thus the *Independent-Mail,* to rethink his position on clever teaser headlines for features and his position on big one-column headlines.

We ought not abandon cleverness, but we must not strive for it at the expense of our ability to give the reader full information. The busy reader must have some idea of the subject before going into a story. Otherwise, he or she is likely to consider that story one of many that will go unread. And all readers are busy readers.

Headline problems go beyond blind heads on features. Some readers look at almost nothing but headlines, and they want to get news from them. You and I want to read the whole newspaper. Readers don't have time. Really. Some can be satisfied by a check of the headlines.

Ginn says he was at first offended by that view. "What right does a reader have to ignore all of our stories and just read the headlines?" he asked. Then he realized that the reader has "a right to do as he pleases" once he gets the paper. (For an eye-opener, Ginn suggests reading one copy of your own newspaper that way—going through and reading nothing but headlines to see whether you get a full picture of the news.)

One final thought on headlines: *Independent-Mail* readers wanted all important parts of the story cited in the head. They did not like finding good material buried. Perhaps that means the old-timers were right when they added decks, kickers, underlines and other ways to run more information in big type.

Years of research show that readers look at photos before anything else on a newspaper page. Then they read the cutlines. Or try to. If we give them only snippets—a name with no ID, for instance—we irritate them. A partial quote with the name does little more for readers, because they have to check the full story before the quote makes sense. I can support the use of a single line of type on a photo that accompanies a story. But that line must carry enough information to make the reader understand the picture.

I was happy to see that the research supports my view on the time element in cutlines. Readers were puzzled by a present-tense sentence that had a date. To wit: *Bobby Unser smashes into the wall Friday.* Drop the time element from that sentence; it belongs in the second or third sentence.

Cutlines and leads got bad marks for wordiness. Ginn narrowed the problem. He went past the number of words to the number of ideas. Readers could follow fairly long sentences that contained only one basic idea. Extra clauses that brought in tangential ideas left readers floundering.

The *Independent-Mail* found one other big problem – inaccuracy. Readers said they put down the newspaper when they run into something they know is wrong. Not only do they put it down, but they don't pick it back up. Not only do they not pick it back up, but they let their subscriptions lapse, too. And now we are getting close to home. We're talking money. We're talking livelihood. We're talking about the influence a newspaper can have. Or not have.

Every newspaper – weekly, small daily, metro monster – should have an error-elimination program. First you identify errors. Then you go after them. John Ginn suggests you have this point of view as you examine copy: "I know there are some errors here; I wonder how many of them I can find and eliminate."

# Writing Headlines
## The Key Word

I do not have to sell you on the importance of headlines. People who read this book have moved along in their careers far enough to have learned that lesson.

So I offer one guideline to help you write headlines: Find the key word in the story and use it in the headline.

Every story has a key word – synonyms count – that must be in the headline. For example, a headline said this: *Inmate accused of murder.* Prison murder happens so often, I regret to say, that it isn't startling news. But the key word would have made this more interesting. The inmate was accused of killing the warden. That word, *warden,* lifts this out of the ordinary into an unusual story. The headline should tell us so.

You must start by finding the key word. Then you must try to be as specific as you can. Take this one: *Accident kills 4 at construction site.* We readers have no way to know precisely what happened. Perhaps a trench collapsed. A building fell on the workers. Paint blew up. They were gassed. Or burned. We don't know. Actually, this appeared on a story about four men who died when a crane's cable broke and they fell 165 feet. So we say: *4 workers fall 165 feet to death.* Or you can skip the height and say: *Cable snaps; fall kills 4 workers.*

After that, you have nothing to do but find the strong verbs and telling adjectives that fit. Headline writers must cultivate the habit of using strong verbs, lively verbs, illuminating verbs. I do not mean words like *blast, flay* and *hit,* the standbys of headlinese (covered later in this chapter). I simply mean you want a precise verb that conveys an image of a specific action.

You need a list for future reference? None exists. Make your own this way:

1. Attack the next edition of your newspaper with a grease pencil.
2. Write in a stronger verb for every headline, even the good ones, in the first 12 pages. Do not worry about the length of your verb; you can struggle with fitting it into the headline some other time.
3. Do the same thing every day for a week, with your own newspaper or some other.
4. After a week, skip the grease pencil and do this exercise only in your mind.
5. After another week, use verbs that fit in the holes left by the verbs you changed. Alternatively, you can adjust the wording in the rest of your practice headlines to allow room for your new, muscular verbs.

You wonder whether grown people would do this sort of thing? Yes. Name a baseball hitting star. He probably makes a million dollars a year. He also takes batting practice. Yes, he gets a million dollars a year, and he's a superior batter already, but he still practices. He gets to bat three to six times every game, but he practices anyway. Why wouldn't a journalist practice? Why wouldn't a journalist be willing to do something for self-improvement?

You have no deadline when you wield the grease pencil. You can take your time and hit only the pitches that come right over the plate. If you don't like the word you choose at first, you get to choose another. Eventually, you get a home-run word. And the more you try this practice, the more likely you are to produce a prize headline at deadline time.

## Padding Is Fatal

While you have the grease pencil out, perhaps you can use it to circle all the useless words you find in headlines. Elimination of padding will give you more room to be specific. Example of padding: *President Bush going home to Texas for Thanksgiving holidays.* I fudged on that one to give you plenty of sinners. You need only one word to identify the person involved; either *President* or *Bush* will handle it. No matter who we have as president, the name alone adequately identifies the person. Then we have *home to Texas.* If we want to emphasize the home angle, we can drop *to Texas.* Otherwise, we can refer to all of that as just *Texas.* (We have a minor problem here, in that Bush grew up in Maine. However, he called Texas home in his political campaigns.) Then we have *Thanksgiving holidays.* This story would run just before the trip, no doubt, so we could use either of the words; we would not need both. All readers would know which holidays we meant. If we just used the word *Thanksgiving,* readers would know we had holidays in mind.

The point: You receive a specified amount of space in which to fit information of great value to readers. You cannot waste any of that room. You have to tell as much as you can as specifically as you can. You have to fashion a lively string of words that will accurately tell people about something of interest to them in the story your headline covers.

And you don't think you ought to practice? Every headline writer should practice.

## Qualification and Attribution

Let's move on to qualification, the process of showing that some outside source, not the writer, stands behind the truth of a statement.

Rule 1: If you qualify the story, you have to qualify the headline.

This holds for inconsequential items as well as major accusations. (Time out for a definition and a distinction. Qualification is the practice of indicating that the newspaper is reporting something from some source but is not necessarily supporting the statement. Attribution is the practice of naming a specific source for the information. Attribution is a higher level of qualification.) We have only one concession. Although the story may attribute a statement of opinion to a specific person, the headline need only indicate that an opinion has been offered; it does not have to be specific. The story can say Joe Doe called Martin Naval a liar. The head can just say he *was called* a liar. Nothing specific. Such a head would be qualified but not attributed. If a headline is attributed, it is automatically qualified.

Rule 1 does not hold for the editorial page. Editorial headlines ought to make an assertion. They need to criticize or praise: *Fire the*

*speaker. Ban the bomb. The Speaker goofs again. The Speaker goofs—
again.* Or, to use a label, *Capital confusion.* (We will get back to that
dash in the goofy headline.)

Incidentally, I would put qualified headlines on columns. Presumably not all your columnists have the same outlook. Without qualification, you might have side-by-side column headlines like these:
*Nixon should be hanged* and *Looks like Nixon was right.* Qualification
prevents that.

Fine. How do we qualify headlines?

Regular verbs do the job best: *Governor termed incompetent.*
That tells us someone has said something bad about the governor.
Another: *Elred accused of stupid moves.* That's OK. It says someone
made an accusation. However, you need to be careful and not step
outside the well-tended path. If you say *Elred criticized for stupid moves,*
you have thrown in an adjective that doesn't belong. The same sort of
thing goes for this one: *Elred's stupidity called a disgrace.* I do not know
Mr. Elred personally, so I cannot vouch for the accuracy of the accusation. However, its accuracy is not in question. What we question is our
right to make such an assertion. The headline assumes Elred's stupidity. And then it tells what someone has said about it. Wrong.

Try another: *Nixon's greatness disputed.* Can't do that, either.
No matter what you think of Nixon, you cannot refer to his greatness,
for that's a judgment call. You could say his stature was disputed or his
place in history was disputed. Everyone has stature. Every president,
even Millard Fillmore, has a place in history.

But greatness must exist before it can be discussed as fact,
and greatness lies in the eye of the beholder. If your politics make the
preceding discussion distasteful, be advised that this headline won't
fly, either: *Nixon's greed debated.*

One other problem lurks in this underbrush: the word *said.*
Newspapers that truly care about literacy and about good headlines
will not abuse that word. Abuse comes in this kind of headline: *Nixon
said greedy. Nixon said splendid. Fire said arson.* No, no, no. You can be
*called* splendid, but people cannot *say* you anything. They cannot say
you slow. They cannot say you hungry. They cannot even say you
down to sleep. (They can say: *Salad said to be key to longevity.* The *to be*
salvages it.)

Let's close with Rule 2: Qualification, if required, must be in
the main part of the headline, not in a kicker or deck or other subsidi-
ary part.

People do not always read kickers and secondary decks. Thus

a headline saying *FBI knew of JFK plot* will startle a lot of people who do not see the kicker, *Starlet thinks.*

## Punctuation

Although we properly put more emphasis on wording, punctuation continues to trouble us in headline writing.

The comma and the semicolon cause most of the trouble. Headline writers get them switched. Let's review. The comma indicates a pause. A semicolon indicates a full stop, the same as a period would do in body type. Commas can also replace the word *and* when we have a compound subject or a compound predicate or even a compound object. Some phrases sound much better with *and*. A reference to a big butter-and-egg man does not have the proper ring if a comma replaces *and*. Ditto in the land of milk, honey.

Here's a compound subject, and it gets a comma: *Nixon, Carter debate.* Predicate: *Elred lies, cheats, steals.* Object: *Elred collects wives, debts.*

Let's look at that again. When we have two subjects and only one verb, we can use a comma:

Newsmen, women deplete city's liquor supply

You can call that a compound subject if you like. Try another compound predicate, still using just a comma:

Newsmen invade city, fill church pews

And the object once more:

Newsmen fill church pews, bars

Of course, you can use two subjects and two predicates in a single independent clause. That will require commas, not a semicolon:

Newsmen, women deplete liquor supply, rue decision

Try one with a comma where it should have nothing:

Student wins suit, but loses his home

No comma. He wins but loses. If we had a *he* before *loses,* a comma would be acceptable but not mandatory, as in: *Student wins suit, but he loses his home.*

Another comma problem:

Braves roll over Cardinals 8-1

I would use a comma, figuring that the *8-1* was sort of parenthetical. It comes as an afterthought to the main idea, that the Braves rolled. A comma looks best in such a headline most of the time. If you consider *8-1* as part of the main description, you can argue that we do not need the comma. That is, we would have the Braves beating the Cards 8-1, like beating them handily. *Beat* is the only verb that comes to my mind for cases like this, although others no doubt exist.

Now we wrestle with misuse of the semicolon. Some newspapers routinely ask that simple mark to do too much work. They want to get two thoughts into the headline, but they want to use one subject and two verbs. For example:

Jones takes over at Ford; was mechanic 10 years ago

I would not cancel my subscription to a newspaper if it committed such a breach; we've all done worse. Indeed, that approach appears on perhaps a majority of the nation's obituary sections. Still, you get a more professional headline if you rearrange: *Jones, a mechanic 10 years ago, takes over at Ford.*

Two more:

Reagan suffers a direct hit; never touched before

This one is a little harder to understand. If we cannot get a subject for the second sentence, the part after the semicolon, we should use a comma and rewrite: *Reagan suffers a direct hit, the first in 6 years.*

Baker shines in one-man show; worked hard to reach stardom

Here, we try to piggyback a half-sentence onto the subject of the first sentence. Give that second sentence its own subject: *Baker shines in one-man show; stardom a long time arriving.*

Another example:

Actress almost strangled by scarf; is saved by cab driver

You cannot use a semicolon there; we have no subject for the second sentence. If the second part said *cab driver saves her,* all would be fine. It doesn't, so it isn't.

We see more semicolon problems in headlines with this construction:

John Jones dies; was Rotary leader

That one will probably get by in half the country's newspapers. I would be much happier with a clause saying *he led Rotary,* or something like that, after the semicolon. And I would draw the line at *John Jones dies; Rotary leader.*

This one needs a hyphen:

Israeli, U.S. tension reported

Although we do indeed refer to *Israeli and U.S. tension,* the hyphen makes a clearer replacement for *and.* It joins the two and says the tension lies between them.

We have other punctuation marks for headlines. Take the dash. Use it as a muscular comma. We had this example in the previous section: *The Speaker goofs again,* as opposed to *The Speaker goofs—again.* The dash adds a great deal of muscle to the final word. It throws special emphasis there. It adds some twist. If you want to take off on a tangent or throw a spotlight on the ending, consider the dash or ellipsis points ( . . . ). Note the strength in these two:

24 Ridley turtles—the rare ones—found on island
Jones told to begin development—or else

Dashes provide a nice touch for headlines—if you don't overdo them.

We also have a friend in the colon. I like it in headlines like this one, my favorite:

Sumo wrestling: survival of the fattest

Some newspapers like to use the colon and the dash in attribution. That works as a last resort, but you can do better with verbs. Oh, I don't get exercised over it in something like this:

Nixon: I'll never try again

You can understand it readily. But you trouble us when you do it this way:

> America cannot rebound: Castro
> America cannot rebound – Castro

You should at least hesitate before using the colon or dash in attribution.

You should also hesitate, if not stop completely, when you try to work wonders with quotation marks. (Newspapers use single quotation marks in headlines.) Some people want to use them to indicate that someone has said something, as in:

> Wildcats to have 'best season in history'

Such a head is on shaky ground. The poor reader has no idea who is making such a statement – the coach, the players or an opponent trying to butter up the Wildcats.

A greater problem arises when newspapers try to fudge with those quote marks. The quoted part has to be a precise quotation, lifted directly from the story. If the story quotes someone as saying he is "100 percent dead sure positive the Aggies will romp and stomp in the Cotton Bowl," we cannot legitimately use a head saying *Aggies 'sure to win' bowl game.*

Editors do that sort of thing in some countries, much to the confusion of readers. And there lies the key to your use of punctuation in headlines: You are supposed to write in such a way that readers will understand you. Readers will not know your esoteric rule that a colon means attribution at the end or that you can use semicolons with only one subject if you have a past-tense verb. Readers will know only what they read, and you must enable them to understand your thoughts quickly.

Let's look now at a questionable mark. Only a desperate copy editor would try to indicate qualification with a question mark. Look at these two:

> Transcript shows entrapment?
> Lakers lose series and center?

What thoughts are supposed to be planted in the reader's mind? Those aren't even real questions. (Real question: *Does transcript show entrapment?*) And if they were, who would be asking them? Do the headlines mean that the newspaper, standing for all fair-minded people, has a question? Or do they mean that someone has made an allegation? The answer here: both. The entrapment headline refers to a lawyer's charge. The other one covers a story that says the center is considering leaving the Lakers.

Prevent such confusion by avoiding question marks except on real questions. I hate to say it, but you see some moderately good newspapers skating through on question-mark heads like those.

Let's turn to parentheses for a final problem. You can probably go through a fairly lengthy career without using parentheses in a headline. They can be confusing. Witness two examples:

> Rangers are (W)right, by George
> Ride (et al.) on!

Down in the first story we learn that a player named George Wright has performed well. But we had to force our cleverness into the headline. Forced cleverness has an odor to it. The second headline was about Sally Ride, the first woman astronaut. It has unnatural phrasing. We might get by with *Ride on!*—even with that exclamation point on the end. The material in parentheses ruins it.

One more. I would accept this:

> Trouble in the Big Apple: Billy Martin on firing line (again)

That set of parentheses does the same thing as the dash noted at the start of this piece. It emphasizes the point. A dash would do the job. Ellipses would be all right, too. Parentheses help. I don't want to say we have only one way to do anything. On the other hand, newspapers have an obligation to be clear, and parentheses do not contribute much to clarity.

## Feature Headlines

No secrets here. No magic keys to creativity. I just propose to discuss feature headlines, dissect a few good ones, and then encourage you to put a little more effort into writing them.

You need good feature heads. They do three things you want done:

1. Catch the reader's eye
2. Entertain readers
3. Convey information

Don't overlook that last one.

Let's look at how all this comes about.

First, we have clever wording in a normal format. We get no typographic tip-offs, just plain heads. I recall one on a story about Mory's Tavern (source of "The Whiffenpoof Song," with its poor little lambs who have lost their way, baa, baa, baa). Mory's was told to admit women or lose its liquor license. The *New York Daily News* had this splendid headline: *Mory's li'l lambs face a ewe turn.*

We'll look at some more of those in a moment. Let's go first to special packaging for still another kind of feature headline.

Feature heads should capitalize on special use of type, special gimmicks, now and then. These range from simple old-fashioned western type on a rodeo feature to computer type on something electronic or an Oriental face on a feature about Chinese cooking.

Then we have reverses, photographic tricks, multiple sizes within one headline, and other gimmickry. A headline on a swimmer's practice regimen said only: *1900 yards a day.* Like this:

# 1900

## yards

# a day

The first and third lines were in bold type, making *1900* and *a day* stand out and then somehow making *yards* stand out, too, by being different.

We also get the magazine approach, in which we set part of a sentence in, say, 18 point, and then hit the last two or three words in 60 point or so. A picture page about auctioneering had *going, going, gone* in big type as the lead headline. But a paragraph in 18-point type led up to it, saying the days of the auctioneer were troubled and some of the old skills were . . . then the three big words, *going, going, gone.*

Generally, this packaging will be done by one person, because the idea comes out as a unit. That is, the story, art and headline must fit together. They support each other. Art can be resized if a headline needs something special. Or a headline can be reworded or resized if we decide a picture should be larger.

Creativity, bolstered by a willingness to steal or just adapt good ideas from other newspapers, will produce this kind of feature headline.

We have no place to steal from when it comes to clever wording in ordinary formats. We have to use our own wits.

Fine. Use them. Get started. Use puns. Use other wordplay. Use whatever it takes to grab readers and keep them. A pun:

> Iced-drink lovers enjoy novel teas

No big deal. Just a simple wordplay.
Try some others:

> Local prostitutes using a few new tricks

That headline, accurate, uses the word *tricks* two ways. Good.

> Freckle queen caught red-headed

Here we have taken a slight twist at the end, producing a wholesome image (in my mind, anyway).

> Porn publisher pursues life, liberty and a buck

Again, we've darted off on a tangent there at the end. This headline comes perilously close to being alliterative with three *p* words at first. Then it settles down. Hint: Always avoid alliteration avidly; it has a ring of forced humor to it.

> Protesters take aim at rifle range

OK, I like this one, but it illustrates a danger. At some point, I am not sure where, we move from cleverness to triteness. The headline writer usually sees that only after everyone else has spotted it. Some people, handling a story, any story, about a canine, will try to say that something has gone to the dogs. Feathered subjects are always for the birds. Dishwashers are in hot water. Be careful. Don't go for the automatics, the ones we write by reflex. Give us some new cliches.

> Police offer drunken drivers a pick-me-up

That gives us a good, soft-sell headline on a serious story. We might try one with a colon, a feature favorite:

> Parent care: guilt-edged bonds

Good pun. I sort of like colon heads on features. The colon replaces a verb, probably the weak *is*.

> Mexico's economy: The fiesta's over

Good. The first two words give us the subject, as they did in the sumo and parent care headlines, and then we get the message. In this case, *fiesta* replaces *party* quite nicely.

> Some loving couples want it in writing
> He left his heart in Odessa, and it relocated
> Pristine forest? It's over there, under that bluish haze
> A cloud of concern hangs over smog tests
> Saturday's favorite food show a picnic for the judges

I like all of those.
Some suggestions:
Be daring. I would rather see you flop with a pun now and then than see you fearful of ever trying.
Be mature. Don't force the humor. Don't call attention to your own cleverness. The headline must make good sense in both its meanings — with wordplay and without it — to be usable.
Be accurate. The story with the *Mory's li'l lambs* headline mentioned "The Whiffenpoof Song" in the lead. The song refers to poor little lambs. That gives the li'l-lamb idea legitimacy. That then gives legitimacy to the ewe-turn angle. *Ewe turn* sounds like *U-turn,* and both make sense. On top of all of that, the headline is accurate no matter how you read it.
Some people have a special talent for this sort of headline

work. You need not despair if you think you do not belong in this category. Cleverness can be learned, though not without effort. You do not have to turn out a snapper on every offbeat story. But if you can write one on occasion, you will brighten your readers' lives—and probably make your own day a little more enjoyable.

Try it.

## Headlinese: Nix on Esoteric Lingo

Although headline writers go about their task differently from newswriters, they have no more latitude when it comes to accuracy and clarity. Indeed, the copy editor's restricted space makes the chore more difficult than newswriting, in some ways.

I wish I could report that all headline writers—we'll call them editors from now on—do a marvelous job of telling the story, selling the story, and pointing out things of interest. They don't. We don't. We are cursed with far too many editors who believe that headlines should be written in some strange jargon, full of short, mysterious words.

Nonsense. Headlines should take a straightforward approach to the news, using familiar language to tell us what we need to know about stories. Let's look at some of the problems that pop up most often in any examination of headlines.

These come to mind, not necessarily in order of importance: identification, repetition, punctuation and qualification (both covered above), and the old standbys, such as split headlines, short counts, abbreviations standing alone and prepositions on the ends of lines.

Identification problems grow from frustration. Newsmakers frequently pass our way only once, and their names, used alone, are not enough to let readers know who they are. Some editors try, and they end up confusing readers. Other editors, unwilling to use an unfamiliar name, fall back on something like *area man*. This reminds me of Clark Kent and his friend: It's a bird, it's a plane, it's . . . Area Man. The problem calls for a bit of thought, for an examination of the the story for some clue as to a word or phrase that will describe Area Man. He may be a victim, a lawyer, a banker, a car salesman—our job is to find a description that will fit the headline and fit the subject.

We can use names when the subject will be clearly recognizable to most readers. Who says it's clear? The news editor, the copy chief—whoever is in charge. That person has to know who in town is recognizable by name and who isn't. Ditto for state and national figures. This knowledge comes with experience, including time spent in the city of publication. Some names come and go in importance and in recognizability. For example, you get no tingle of recognition when I use the name *Whitman,* possibly excluding those of you who like country music. But let's look at a series of headlines, run day by day, that built toward the name.

**Texas sniper kills 16 from tower**

**Tower sniper survivor tells of surprise**

**Sniper's plans found**

**Whitman once youngest Eagle Scout**

**Whitman's friends still can't believe it**

Headlines evolve that way. We start with a tower sniper, cut that to a plain sniper, and soon, after the name has been in the news more than a day, call him by name. Then, 20 years later, we start with the assumption that no one has ever heard of him. The name won't do. It means nothing without some context.

One other problem with names. We sometimes have more than one person with the same name in the news. In 1987 we had Bo Jackson, Reggie Jackson, Jesse Jackson and maybe one more in the news. On the sports pages, *Bo* was satisfactory, though in other parts of the paper *Bo* could be Diddley or Jangles. You can get by with context; a headline saying Jackson was looking for votes would presumably apply only to Jesse.

Still, we have to think about these things as we write headlines.

I mentioned repetition. Repetition slips in too often when an editor finds a snappy phrase in the story. If the editor steals that snappiness from the lead, the reporter is entitled to punch the editor in the nose. No lead is clever enough to overcome the handicap of repetition. Stealing the lead for a headline is like stepping on the punch line in someone's joke. You do so only at the risk of incurring eternal hatred.

And deserving it.

Now for a slap at headlinese before we stop. You recognize headlinese instinctively, even if you have never seen that word. It comes in words like *slated, parley, blast, rip, flay, solon, ink* and *eye.* Its use exposes a beginner at once. Veterans do not have to stoop to that. Some do, but only out of ignorance. (A friend of mine claims to know a sportswriter who uses words like that in regular conversation. This chap is supposed to have said once that a softball teammate laid a bunt on the rug and outlegged an underarm heave to the initial hassock.) If people used headlinese in normal conversation or even normal reading, I would not object to its use in the newspaper. But we should not use words that show up nowhere but crossword puzzles and weak headlines.

That leaves us with just a few rules to cover. I try to blanket beginning headline writers with all the rules. If they can write under restrictions, they will have no trouble if they get some leeway. For example, I require that all lines be within two counts of the maximum. That keeps people from turning in whatever comes to mind. If a trained editor wants to violate that rule after showing an ability to live with it, I won't quarrel for a minute. But I would make that a basic goal for newspapers, hoping to avoid raggedness.

Split heads bother me more than short counts, mainly because some of them mislead readers. The reader may think an adjective is a noun. Look at two:

Wealthy
lawyer
indicted

Soviet virgin
lands program
brought to end

The first would grieve no one, for *wealthy* is much more likely to be considered an adjective than anything else. (*The wealthy* would be another matter.) The second headline throws us off, because *virgin* looks like a noun. Then we hit the bottom line and see that *virgin* has gone from noun to adjective. Readers would not be overcome with pique, but they would be misled just a little. We ought not mislead them at all.

# Writing Cutlines

I seem to have misplaced my stone tablets, so we will have to go with something less authoritative in this discussion of cutlines. As a matter of fact, you won't find thoughts about cutlines engraved on stone anywhere. Sometimes I think we don't even have words about them written on paper. The world's newspapers go their separate ways on this subject.

Fine. I don't want to dictate. But I do want to offer some thoughts about cutlines, because cutlines make a strong contribution to reader pleasure. You need not agree with the wisdom that begins in the next paragraph, but you ought to at least think about cutlines and be sure you know why you want to follow some other path.

Cutlines ought to do four things: They should explain the action, name the principals, tell why we're running the photo, and note details the reader might overlook. You may want to add one more function: identify the source.

We have two main kinds of cutlines: full and skeleton. Full lines normally run with photos that have no accompanying story—wild art, it's often called. Skeleton lines normally run with art that has an accompanying story. Some newspapers insist on running full lines with all art. That practice has one good point and one bad, with the bad outweighing the good. On the plus side, full lines make it easier to explain the picture enough to help the reader and thus increase readership. However, that same goal can be reached with skeleton lines produced by a skillful writer. On the bad side, full lines too often duplicate information contained in the accompanying story. Readers are put off by reading the same thing twice. And if the idea is also contained in the headline, we have a bored reader before the second paragraph comes up. Skeleton lines, properly done, identify the principals and explain the action as briefly as possible.

Full lines normally start with what I call the main descriptive sentence. This one tells us what we are seeing. If we see two guys shaking hands, it does not—well, it shouldn't—tell us they are shaking hands. It tells us one is congratulating the other or saying goodbye or welcoming him to the team. Don't state the obvious; just tell us what the obvious means. Don't tell us the baseball player waves his hand; tell us he acknowledges cheers for a home run or a good catch or a triumph in salary negotiations.

Remember that the main descriptive sentence tells us, in present tense, what is happening in the photo. Why present tense? Well, the photo shows some action frozen for all time. Therefore, we say the player *acknowledges* instead of *acknowledged.* We drop the time element out of the sentence, too. In skeleton lines, we drop the time element altogether. In wild lines, we slip it into another sentence. That second sentence might say something like this: *The Astros' catcher had four hits Thursday in a 6-0 victory over Chicago.*

You do not have to have a separate sentence for each of the four functions. Most of the time, the reasons for running a picture will be obvious. But on car wreck pictures, for example (and we have too many such examples), your main descriptive sentence is likely to say that fire fighters clean up or pull the victim out of the car, or something like that. You will have a sentence or a clause that says four people were hurt – our reason for running the art.

As for citing details readers might overlook, I recall one picture in which a principal was wearing a cast on her foot. It was not prominent, but cutlines pointed it out and explained it, as an item of interest for readers.

Cutlines should identify everyone who is clearly recognizable and who is part of the main action. You need not identify all the Secret Service men walking with the president, even though they are identifiable. If one of those men catches the president's falling hat (assuming he wears a hat), you should identify him; he has become part of the main action.

How do you handle identification? We have four main ways: obviousness, action, position, elimination. If you have a picture of four people and one is the governor and he is at a desk and a sign on his desk tells us his name, you do not need to say which one he is. Obviousness. If you have two people and only one has a woman's name and if only one person in the photo wears a dress, you do not need to do anything further; that's also obviousness. The next one, action, is pretty simple, too. If someone opens a car door for the president, you identify the person through the action. If a person is scrambling out of the way in the photo, you do not need to say *in battle gear* in this cutline: *Secretary of State Al Haig, in battle gear, jumps aside as the president leaves. . . .* Just the action will cover it.

You know about position. It is probably the most common identifier: *Al Haig, left, greets an old Army buddy, Blackjack Pershing. . . .*

And that brings us to elimination. Let's say we have four principals in a scene. One is behind a desk with his name on it. We recognize him as our governor. That's obviousness. He is shaking hands with another fellow, Joe Smith. We mention the congratulations to new aide Smith; that's action. Then we tell what the other two guys are doing this way: *Speaker Gib Lewis, left, and Lt. Gov. Bill Hobby, both Smith supporters, wait to offer their welcome.* We took care of Lewis by position, left. That leaves only Hobby, the fourth fellow we show. By elimination, the one next to the end is Hobby.

Fun, eh?

Let's try some fun on catch lines. Catch lines are those little headlines on full cutlines. Some people use little headlines and others use boldface capital lines set into the cutlines type. I prefer the former. Either way, they are valuable. Really. Research says so. You can help readers a great deal with good catch lines. We want clever lines, even funny lines if the subject is not morbid, but we need to put clarity first. Your goal is to help readers understand the photo quickly. An American Society of Newspaper Editors study dealt with a photo of a car that smashed into a store. One suggested line, moderately cute, said: *A new drive-in.* A better one, if we're after understanding, said: *He hit the wrong pedal.*

So, be clever. Be funny when humor fits. Use rhymes. Use puns. But above all, tell the reader something about the photo.

Is there a correct format for cutlines? Not really. Some things work better than others, but you, as editor, have to decide what you like and then go with it. My intention is to remind you of your options.

We will tackle this from two directions: form and content.

Cutlines should stand out from body type. They will if you set them 1 or 2 points larger. A switch to sans serif type also makes them stand apart from body type. If you have no small sans serif type, you can use boldface roman. My preference, considering no limitations, would be 11 on 12 sans serif, fairly bold. (Type need not be named bold to be bold. Futura Bold is too black for cutlines, for instance, but Futura Medium is satisfactorily bold. Futura is not an ideal type for cutlines.) Sometimes, you can set cutlines in your headline face; you have to decide whether the face is too strong or hard to read.

I would not use italic except in one-line cutlines, if anywhere. Single lines, often all caps (but better in caps and lowercase), usually work well on pictures accompanying stories. If your art is with a story, don't wear your readers out by repeating all the information from the story; use only enough to explain the picture.

The best arrangement is to line up cutline margins with the edges of your art. That makes the package look a little more unified. Cutlines that have two or more legs of type should have 12 to 24 points between segments. I like 18. A gap of less than 12 points cramps the type; more than 24 gives you a chasm to cross.

Some newspapers run legs no wider than their body type, say 14 picas. That seems short to me. I can accept lines up to about 30 picas wide. That means only two columns (25½ picas) on the modern format. I would use a single leg on one- and two-column cuts, two legs on three and four columns, and three legs on five and six columns.

The easiest way to handle the credit line (for example, *−AP LaserPhoto* or *−Facts Photo by Jim Trotman*) is to run it at the end of the cutline and in the same type. That approach, though functional, is less attractive than just a 6-point line at the lower right corner of the picture, above the cutlines. If credit lines are run in as part of the cutline copy, they should be at the end, set flush right. If the last line is too long to permit you to set the credit line without breaking it over to another line, move it all to that next line, still setting it flush right. You don't have this problem if you use the 6-point line at the corner.

You have four ready options for catch lines: 1. Forget catch lines and go right into the lines. 2. Use a headline-size line above or to the left of your cutlines. 3. Use a read-in. 4. Use a read-through.

The available research indicates that an introductory line of some sort can make an appreciable difference in the way a reader understands a photograph. So we scratch No. 1. My preference— barely—is an 18- to 24-point catch line centered above the cutlines. Flush left is also acceptable. As far as that goes, on a picture four columns wide or more, you could set the catch line on the same level with, but to the left of, the cutlines themselves. Although catch lines add pleasing white space, they take up more room than other formats. You may be reluctant to yield that space.

That takes us to the read-in, which I define as an all-cap phrase or long word at the beginning of cutlines, a phrase that reads right into the lines. For example:

AN AGING PROFESSOR in Austin sits forlornly at his typewriter. . . .

I prefer our next option, the read-through, to the read-in. A read-through, to me, is a boldface all-caps phrase or long word placed at the beginning of cutlines but not part of the sentence:

**EDITOR HORSEWHIPPED**—Country editor Martin Elred displays stripes from a whipping he suffered. . . .

Now, the trick on catch lines is to be informative first and clever second. Everybody loves clever photo captions. But your main goal is to pass along information so the reader can pick up what is happening. Do not be funny at the expense of the flow of information.

# 10

# Layout and Design

Layout I: helping readers • *Massive grayness. Bumping headlines. Other bumping elements. Inadequate art display. Improperly positioned art. Improper headline format.* Layout II: a blank canvas • Jumping • Quality by design • Graphic ideas • Saluting the flag

## Layout I: Helping Readers

This chapter isn't meant to introduce you to layout. That chore is handled by others elsewhere. I only want to give you some encouragement and to offer you some things to think about as you do your work.

Layout plays an important part in newspaper work. Great stories can go unread if they lie hidden in unattractive makeup. You have to get readers to start a story, at least, before you can hold them. Of course, the greatest layout in the world will not sustain a newspaper if it has no content. People read for content, but they need help. The person doing the layout provides that help.

Layout people go at their task a number of ways, with a number of goals. The best ones simply set out to help readers understand the significance of material being spread before them.

Those people capitalize on reader habits at every opportunity. It helps if they know what habits their readers have.

I once worked on a newspaper that, on a big news day, would use an 8-96 (an 8-column, 96-point headline—everyone used eight-column layout in those days) with a readout on the right side; and an 8-72, above the 8-96, with a readout on the left side; and an 8-60 under the

96, reading out God knows where in the middle of the page. We thought readers knew the code because we knew it.

Insight and reflection lead me to believe we fooled a lot of people, including ourselves, with that approach.

This does not mean you cannot help readers develop habits. It means, though, that you must decide what you want those habits to be, and then stick with them. If you use italic headlines only on featurish material, don't switch suddenly and use it on an ax murder. If you want a box to indicate that a story has some offbeat aspects, don't sprinkle boxes throughout the paper every time you want to avoid headline bumps. Some people use boxes only to keep from having heads bump into each other. They remind me of Rocky Marciano—they will box anything. I lean toward the former approach—box only the oddball— but that's just a personal preference.

Another habit involves placement of the lead story. To me, the lead story must run under the nameplate. You can put good material above the flag, but it must be an off-lead or a special feature. I sort of like type that is a little bolder on the lead head, too, although that is not vital. Some type families have no black version. For instance, Bodoni goes from bold (which is only medium heavy) to Ultra Bodoni, which is a different, hyper-ugly family of its own. No matter how you do your job, be consistent.

While we are here in the nunnery, talking about habits, let's check on the sin situation. Six major sins in newspaper layout come to mind. I would have to push to get a list of 10, although I suspect readers will remind me of three, or a dozen, that I should have on the roll. Please do.

1. Massive grayness
2. Bumping headlines
3. Other bumping elements
4. Inadequate art display
5. Improperly positioned art
6. Improper headline format

## Massive Grayness

Otherwise known as elephant's disease (long, gray legs), gray masses give all of us problems on all pages, no matter what kind of layout we have. Modular layout is especially susceptible. (*Modular* is a fancy word we use to describe layout done in rectangles.) It calls for flat bottoms on all stories, keeping you from thrusting headlines of other stories into a block of type to break up the grayness. If a lead story has a three-column headline and 18 inches of type, you have a 3-by-6 area of grayness. I don't get nervous until we get 20 inches—3 by 7, say, or 4 by 5. The problem worsens on big inside pages, where we run a 4-by-10 chunk on occasion.

I encourage you to attack this problem with vigor. Here are some suggestions for breaking up grayness, in order of my preference. Wiser people may have other ideas or different priorities.

BOLD CAP READ-INS

Give these 6 points of space above, every four paragraphs or so, and you lighten a page. These were in vogue for a while and then faded. I see them some nowadays.

SUBHEADS

These work best on, say, a half-page spread with wide type. A 14-point subhead preceded by 6 to 12 points of space will let some air into a gray mass. Those old subheads we used to run, in bold body type, were useful then, but they lack the elegance of a one- or two-line subhead in larger type. You would not run both bold-cap read-ins and subheads.

INITIAL CAPS TO OPEN A PARAGRAPH

Big initials, three lines deep, also preceded by 6 to 12 points of space, help a lot, though they are troublesome to set. They can be set into three indented lines, or they can be aligned with the bottom of only the paragraph's opening line, leaving the rest of the cap sticking up. The part sticking up introduces white space.

INSET QUOTES

These look good, but they have a drawback. If you run them between fairly heavy lines, or if your type is black, or if you run them long, they tend to turn the reader's eye back to the next column. A fairly light type, 12- or 14-point, with rules no more than 3 points thick, will do nicely. And don't run them more than five lines long.

Some people break up single-column matter with two-column reader quotes. Horrible! I invariably find my eye bouncing back to the top instead of reading through. Do not ask that much of your readers. I would rather see 72-point initial caps. One newspaper I read even uses color blocks on the quotes. No one could smash through that barrier.

HALF-COLUMN MUGS

We used to run these, but they did nasty things to type in narrow columns. We might use some in today's wider measures. I still prefer a half-column mug matched by the subject's name in the other half column, rather than running the regular text half a column wide. Eyes can go right through a barrier so light, but it breaks up the grayness.

Whatever you do, don't float a one-column mug in a column of type. Such a photo will bump the reader's eye to the next column every time.

## Bumping Headlines

Modern layout often produces bumping headlines. I can forgive that, but only if you set things up so the bumping appears to be on purpose. You fall from grace when headlines in adjoining columns have half an inch or so of vertical space between them. That looks accidental. If you must bump, do it on purpose. Line your headlines up, and get your separation by running the heads in a different number of lines, increasing the type size of one head by 12 to 18 points over the other, or using different typefaces. You can also box one story. No matter how you do it, a pair of three-column headlines lined up across a page will not be splendid. Bump cleanly or not at all.

## Other Bumping Elements

Mainly, this refers to the placement of a boxed story next to a photo or an ad. A photo beside an ad always runs a risk of having to compete with a halftone in the ad. Even a dark ad with nothing but type will compete. Try to keep them apart, although you should not commit some other sins in your effort. A box causes the same problem. If a photo runs next to a box, neither stands out.

## Inadequate Art Display

This is not really a makeup problem, but it's common enough to warrant mention. Every newspaper ought to make a strong effort to get better reproduction and then to get good art from photographers and then to play it big. Maybe bigger than that.

## Improperly Positioned Art

We have abundant research to indicate that people looking at newspaper pages think pictures go with stories immediately under them. I encourage you to capitalize on that natural habit; put the art over the story. If it has to be on the side, as it may on inside pages, at least get the headline over the art and the story. I would not use this as a hard-and-fast rule – relax it in packages such as boxes – but I would make it a goal.

If you are looking for a truly bad place to put a piece of art, especially a mug shot, try the first column of a story, with the lead under it. Evidence indicates that people try to start reading where body type touches a headline, and a mug shot in the first column messes things up.

Take advantage of our psychological traits by putting the art over the story if you can. If you can't, at least be sure you have it lined up with the story on three planes (across the top, across the bottom, and the shared plane between them).

## Improper Headline Format and Size

Sometimes we doze and come up with pages that contain nothing but, say, two-line multicolumn headlines. Or all one-liners. You need some variety in format as well as in size. You have two-liners as the basic format, probably, but you ought to throw in a one-liner and something with a kicker or underline now and then. Variety helps.

I don't believe I could bring myself to use italic type on a lead story, but I would not reserve it for features only. I would use it for variety, with two or three roman heads for every italic one.

Depending on your street sales competition and your general desire to do some shouting, you have all kinds of options in choosing type sizes. If you like the big stuff, fine by me. I go for moderation. A 60-point headline or maybe a 72 strikes me as quite large for most days. You might even hold it to 48 for a home delivery sheet.

Oh, you could even start under 48, but that would limit you in how you show differences between the day's stories. That is, a lead head of 42 points means you can dip only two sizes before you get into some pretty small stuff for a six-column page. I don't think a three-line 1-24 can carry a story in the top half of a six-column page.

Still, the main goal is to be consistent, so that a plane crash on the East Coast gets the same size head as we gave to a similar crash in

Iowa last month. (This doesn't hold true if you publish near either crash site or if it has another local connection.)

Actually, I don't mean all equal crash stories get equal play. One will get a better treatment if it happens on a slow news day. However, even then you should have some consistency. The reader should be able to tell, though not precisely, how you weigh today's stories against yesterday's. Or how you weigh today's stories against each other.

And your inside pages ought to continue the consistency. You don't want all your pages to look alike, but you don't want to let one page be led by a wide 72-point screamer while another page with news just as strong is led by something in 36.

We don't whip all these problems every day, but we don't whip any of them unless we make an effort. Happy effort.

# Layout II: A Blank Canvas

A big chunk of education involves the illumination of options. That is, people get educated when they learn they have choices and when they learn they are not limited to choices other people have thought up.

Take layout.

You have a six-column layout sheet. You know when you pick it up that you can do as you wish with it. Good. But you need to remember that your $650-a-ton newsprint does not have a six- or eight- or nine-column layout built in; it's blank. It's a clean surface. You may need to remember this blankness when you start work.

You work within the normal six-column framework, for the sake of convenience. But you have a blank canvas, awaiting your strokes of art. You do not have to follow tradition.

The University of Texas' student newspaper once ran a photo layout sideways on a page, with a lot of reverse type. Odd. Maybe weird. But eye-catching. I would gag on a regular diet of such antics, but I applaud the willingness to take a flier now and then. You might be surprised, too, at what you would produce if told you had to reinvent your newspaper.

And then we have cutlines.

I have had occasion lately to examine cutlines in a bunch of newspapers with which I maintain friendly relations. The quality of their cutlines ran from mediocre to horrid. That makes them typical.

Some of us never sit down and look at the options we have on cutlines—typeface, size, margins, headlines, space between columns and so on. We do what we have always done, which may trace us back to a policy established when we all set type in metal.

You realize that photos draw more attention than anything else on a newspaper page. Readers go to them first. We need to exploit that strength by enhancing photos with good, attractive cutlines. I won't try to decide what's attractive, for that's personal. But I will urge you to examine—I mean take a hard look at—your lines to see if they stand apart from body type, if they are big enough to be read easily, if they line up with the picture's edge to form a unit, if they have clear catch lines (headlines) or bold-cap read-ins, and if they are set some width other than that of your body type. This subject got deeper treatment in the preceding chapter.

# Jumping

The world record for jumped stories is 18, set by the *New York Times* in 1976.

Oh, maybe that's not the record, but it's the most I recall seeing. And it's a darn sight more than most readers will put up with gladly. A study done for the American Society of Newspaper Editors tells us clearly that readers are less than enthusiastic about jumps. (A jumped story is one continued from one page to another.) *USA Today's* success has been based in part on an appeal to short attention spans—offering many stories, few of them long.

Let's start at square one in this discussion. If you have 18 stories on Page 1, you reflect the idea that a little story on Page 1 is worth more than longer treatment inside. I do not intend to argue with that philosophy, though my preference runs to the use of fewer Page 1 stories. A newspaper with, say, five stories outside ought to be able to hold all five to Page 1 unless they are exceptionally long. Seems to me the best policy is to try to eliminate all jumps—but not to try so hard that you work yourself into a corner. You would not want to gut a story just to go along with an arbitrary policy.

Aside from that, we have other considerations affecting jumps. One is length. You err if you jump only the last paragraph or so. Similarly, you ought to use more than just a teaser on Page 1. I once saw a story that jumped from Page 1 after only three lines. Shameful. Readers barely learned what the story was about before they had to go inside.

The next problem is your choice of jump page. The best is the back page of the section. After that comes Page 2, and then Page 3, because they are the next most convenient. Page 2 may not work if you want it for some other special use. Some small newspapers facing tough metro opposition use Page 1 for local stories and put their best wire copy on Page 2 or 3 as a sort of second front page.

Regardless of page choice, you should strive for consistency – the same place every issue. Your goal is to make the reader's job easier. Part of the reader's task is to turn back to Page 1 after reading a jump. We have some evidence that readers who follow a jumped story on an inside page often choose not to come back to Page 1. You don't want that reaction. If readers have to open only one page or flip to the back of the section, getting back to Page 1 is relatively painless.

Other no-nos:

1. Don't jump from one section to another. A newspaper with two sections often gets split up when more than one person reads it, and few stories are so interesting that a reader will wait for a section that has been taken to another part of the house. You know which part.

2. Don't jump from one inside page to another. A possible exception would be from a left-hand page to the one facing it.

3. Don't jump backward. You see backward jumps now and then, usually from a tabloid's back page to the inside. Tabloids that use the back page like a Page 1 showcase for sports can get away with that kind of jumping, perhaps, but it confuses readers of broadsheets.

OK, we have set up our policy. We will jump one or maybe two stories if we have to, and we will go to the back page of the section. What next? Well, we have to guide the reader somehow. I call the necessary line the *see* line, as in *See STORM, Page 2.* You can use whatever pleases you: *Continued on Page 16,* or maybe *Please turn to Page 2, Column 4.* Readers forget the column numbers, though, and are better off with direction to a headline word.

I prefer the *see* line in bold type, centered, in parentheses and with 6 points of white space above it.

You have some choices in jump headlines. You may use a single word or just a phrase as a label. You can write a full headline. One newspaper uses the *see* line's word as a kicker to a regular headline.

One trick that works with all kinds of jump heads is to put a star or other identifying device just to the left of the first head word. Big dots (sometimes called bullets or meatballs) are fairly popular. Many newspapers use a darkened map of Wyoming.[1] Some use three dots. Whatever the device, it should be big enough to catch the eye.

---

1. The state almost forms a square.

As for the head itself, labels are the easiest to write, obviously, and are favored by a majority of newspapers. You can set them up in a hurry, using type of 24 to 48 points. Their disadvantage is that they do little to improve the appearance of a page. A page with nothing but label heads and a few stars is going to be on the gray side. You can overcome this grayness with photos, inset quotes and reader graphics. Moreover, you could place a 2-point border (cutoff rule) after the label and extend it over all the columns of the jump. The cutoff, set against a background of white space the depth of the jump head, opens up the gray mass satisfactorily. You may want to cut a continuation line (the one saying *From Page 1*) into the rule, near the label.

Most newspapers properly put their continuation lines at the beginnings of jumps. Some put them in a rounded box, either a thin rule surrounding regular type or a full reverse. Either idea will work. (The *New York Times* gives you the column number in the *see* line and then the continuation line tells you what column you came from on Page 1. You don't need all that.)

Now and then you see a newspaper that boxes all jumps in one box and uses some reference to continuation for the whole package.

Full headlines for jumps dress up a page quite a bit more than labels do, but they take more time. They are also much more likely to attract readers who missed the story on Page 1. If you use full headlines, try to repeat the key words from Page 1 headlines. Some newspapers try to use the same headline, verbatim, although that can be tough on copy editors if the jump head is in fewer columns.

Let's summarize now, with the gospel according to Saint Red. Remember, dissent is not treated as heresy.

1. Hold down the number of jumps. Eliminate them if you can without distorting news values.

2. Jump to the back page of the section, or to Page 2 or 3, the easy-to-find pages. And use the same page every issue.

3. Don't jump just a smidgin of type, and don't jump everything but the first paragraph.

4. Use label heads, at least 24 points deep on a short jump, going up in size with length of jump. Stretch a border of some sort over all the type in the jump, with white space above and below the line. If you have nothing but a jump on a page, lighten the page up some way (art, from a half-column up, or inset quotes, for example).

5. If you use regular headlines on jumps, word them much like the Page One head.

6. Don't get your page numbers mixed up. OK, so I haven't discussed that yet. Sorry. The readership study I mentioned indicated

that people get teed off because papers give them bum instructions on jumps. They do not like jumps in the first place, and page mistakes gall them no end. Don't you think your readers are too nice for such lousy treatment?

# Quality by Design

Members of the Society of Newspaper Design run on the friendly side. They share their information freely. I enjoy their meetings.

They see that newspaper readership is not rising as fast as population, and they believe that packaging has some effect on that readership. Of course it does, but content has more effect. People are going to read newspapers because they contain information of value. Your job on layout is simply to make that information easier to get to, easier to extract.

One way to make things easier is to offer readers more graphic elements. Pictures, you know about and use lavishly. Maps and charts, you know about but don't use. Why? Why don't we use more charts and maps and graphics in newspapers?

Newspaper designers often think first of the staff artists when they start their planning. Weekly editors get lost there, for most newspapers don't have staff artists. A few weeklies have people who can draw, but that's probably a coincidence.

Maybe so, but this does not mean weeklies cannot run maps and charts. Inexpensive microcomputers, such as the popular Macintosh, let anyone draw charts. You can use a simple bar graph to show how county tax revenues have gone up (or down) in comparison with county employees' pay, for example. Or you can draw a graph of county expenditures on roads through the years. You can even draw a pie chart if you want to show—dramatically—what percent of the budget goes for streets, salaries, bonded indebtedness or what have you.

Maps? Sure, you can have maps. Maps do not have to be topographical masterpieces. Almost all computers have programs that draw a simple map, and a little type can dress it up and show the location of the new sewer line or highway or high school or oil well.

One of the beauties here is that a basic map can be reused if you take off the type and the arrows or X's or lines or whatever designates what you are showing. If you get a good map showing your county's precincts, for instance, you can use it for years, until the boundaries change, if they ever do. On an election story, you can either shade the precincts to show how they voted, or if the map is large enough, you can insert type to show the vote. (Hint: Draw the map big and reduce it.)

Now, back to the central question: Why bother, when you can get across the same idea in words? Well, some information lends itself to graphic portrayal better than to words. Some information is easier to grasp in charts than in paragraphs. These are the things that you—small towns as well as in cities—can do with just a little effort. You can help readers get information a little quicker, a little easier. And that is what helps you maintain readership.

# Graphic Ideas

More readers will look at an informational graphic—such as a map or chart—in your newspaper if you boost the size from one column to two. You can also increase readership by going from black and white to color.

Common sense tells you all that.

But common sense does not tell you how much gain those changes make, nor what effect size and color have on perception of importance and accuracy.

Sarah Caskey tells you.

Caskey got a master's degree in journalism at the University of Texas. She used informational graphics as a thesis topic. (So you'll know: I offered her the benefit of my vast insight. That makes me, and this report, biased. But we're not selling anything.)

Every newspaper, from the smallest weekly to *USA Today,* can use maps and other graphic devices. Blank maps can be kept on hand for a city, a town, a county, even a state. Then when something happens, you can produce an instant map by typesetting names for a couple of streets or some other locater name for a county or state. An X or starburst or square or arrow shows people right where the action occurred.

There you have one purpose of a graphic device: You give readers a big piece of information in a small package. You tell people part of the story quickly. You make something easier to understand.

I applaud that, whether you use a simple map, a fancy drawing, a plain box for a sidebar, or a 1-2-3 listing of a city council's votes.

Graphic items have another major purpose: attracting attention. They do it well. Readership jumps sharply with the addition of a device, especially a photograph. A big photo does even better.

If you get readers to stop on your page for one story, you get a chance to hold them there for a while. Then you offer them other goodies, other stories, with the hope that they will read the whole page. Though we old word lovers hate to give up space for something as frivolous as a photo or a drawing, we're learning. We're learning that tiny pictures with tiny faces won't stop readers as they whiz through the paper. We're learning that if we arrange spectacular stories on a hopelessly ugly page, our spectacular stories will go unread. A newspaper full of wonderful but unread material does its job no better than an airhead newspaper with nothing worth reading.

You are not hearing a call for *National Enquirer* supermarket-special headlines. You are not being urged to capture the rainbow with the *USA Today* approach. Lurid headlines and a megacolor weather map will thrill some people, but most of us can get by without them. We do like *USA Today*'s other informational graphics, however. They provide information for people who do not have time to get it through more conventional ways. *USA Today* graphics would be good in black and white. You can find an idea worth stealing if you look just a little bit.

Caskey will help you decide what to steal. She looks at all kinds of graphics and influencing factors, especially color and size. Let me summarize her main points:

1. Size helps. A two-column map will be much better read than a one-column map. It will also be perceived to be more important and more accurate. The gain in ability to attract attention will be greater than the gain in perception of importance and accuracy. The jump from one column to two will exceed by far the increase from two to three or from three to four.

2. One-column maps do a good job of imparting information and enhancing views of accuracy and importance. They must be done well, with legible type and other features. Do not shrink a map beyond the point of understanding, but do not think you have to take up the whole page with one drawing.

3. Reader attention jumps sharply when you add color to a map. Extra colors will help little; a four-color map gets only a dab more attention than a two-color map.

4. Color has almost no influence on perception of importance and accuracy. Its main contribution, again, is to catch the eye. Color does not help in retention of information.

5. Women have a stronger response to color than men do. If you do not see something important in that statement, you are in the wrong line of work.

# Saluting the Flag

It is not my nature to be disrespectful of the flag, you understand. But now and then I run across a newspaper flag that truly deserves the Rodney Dangerfield treatment—no respect at all.

My bedrock premise in this discussion is that the flag is the most important printing element on your front page. The news comes and goes, but your flag stands for something constant. That, of course, is your integrity, honesty and general ability to put out a newspaper for your town. You ought to watch Chicago commuters buying newspapers. Those people don't look at headlines; they take a *Tribune* or a *Sun-Times* automatically, because they know that the flag is on a paper that carries the news they want and need. Your flag does the same thing in your town.

So why don't you pay more attention to it?

The flag ought to be a clean, tasteful, appropriate piece of ornamentation. If you want to float it and use it as a makeup element, that's fine. I wouldn't float it around the page in every issue, but an occasional move, for a purpose, is perfectly proper.

Let's look at those criteria: clean, tasteful, appropriate. My reference to clean nameplates is meant to suggest that you ought to get most of the gimmickry out of them. To do that, you look at every line, every particle on the flag. Think how the flag would appear without that ink. For instance, many newspapers I looked at for this piece put cutoff rules above and below the folio lines. That upper rule normally has no value; it just adds clutter.

By *clean,* I also refer to extra wording. One newspaper has three mottoes. Another lists the nine towns in its circulation area. A few have ads. I can live with some of that stuff, but I suggest you look at all of it carefully and see if you do want to cleanse yourself. Most of it should be scrapped.

Finally, *clean* refers to excessive ornamentation. I used to tease a friend about all the ornamentation on his newspaper: The flag showed a vista across a valley in which the deer and antelope played amid oil wells and windmills and maybe a cantaloupe patch in bloom. He changed to a computerlike type, often run in reverse, which looked worse, though it was cleaner than the old one. He has since changed again, for the better.

I have in front of me a newspaper with a picture of a big bull, a bale of cotton and a harvesting machine going through a scraggly field of corn or sorghum. That's too much. The people there know they are in farming country; you don't need to remind them three ways. Use your space for other things.

The two other criteria are related to cleanliness. I won't go into taste much, other than to say that the flag ought to be large enough to be seen but small enough to let other elements make a contribution to the page. A big, deep flag inside a thick border is indiscreet. You do not need to shout that much.

As for appropriateness, I ought to mention that the rural scene mentioned above, though perhaps overdone, was indeed fitted to the area, probably better than the computer type. It carried a message, and that's one of the main jobs.

# 11

## The Role of the Newspaper

Credibility ● *Monitor. Supermarket. Reading ease. Open ads. The world. Challenge. Opinion. Opinion page. Advantage. Ethics. Friendship.* Opinion writing ● *We need more. Variety.* Help from outside ● The letters column ● Reviews

## Credibility

Robert S. McCord, associate editor of Little Rock's *Arkansas Gazette,* dropped by the schoolhouse where I work and shared some of his thoughts about newspaper credibility. Bob, visiting as part of the editor-in-residence program, listed 11 things that can help newspapers achieve credibility. His list:

1. Monitor government at all levels.
2. Be a supermarket, with something for everyone.
3. Be easy to read.
4. Open advertising to all.
5. Cover the world as well as the nation.
6. Challenge the concentrations of power within the community.
7. Separate the opinion from the news.
8. Have an opinion page.
9. Avoid taking advantage of your position.
10. Conduct yourself ethically.
11. Be a friend.

We will go over those one by one.

## Monitor

We accept the role of monitor. The ordinary citizen cannot spend days prying into the work of people who handle our tax money, who build our roads, who erect and run our hospitals. The news media must be the reader's surrogate. We have to tell people how their elected representatives voted—whether they be on school boards or in Congress. Within the limits of our resources, we have to be newspapers of record—certainly recording important events of our area, if not the world.

## Supermarket

We cannot be for the rich only. Or for labor unions only. Or only the poor. The old. The sick and lame. We have to have news about the symphony as well as the pepper-eating contest. We cover gospel singers and western yodelers. We cover religion and banking, not to mention youths and their problems. All these things have a place in our newspapers.

## Reading Ease

We have an obligation to save our readers time and effort. We eliminate or cut down drastically on jumps, which few people read anyway. We pick a convenient, regular jump page. We open up the first few pages. We give people a good index; even weeklies need to indicate what can be found inside the paper. We group the news logically, and we take advantage of reader habits. We provide summaries, including, but not stopping at, briefs columns. If, for example, we have three columns of type on a story about the city council, we summarize that material in a sidebar next to or under the main headline. Readers eager to find a single subject can then tell that the story has something for them without having to wade through it all.

## Open Ads

We have to realize—and most do—that advertising has an importance beyond that of bringing in money. We want to make sure that everyone has access to the ad columns, excluding only the illegal ad and the blatant violation of good taste. Yes, we have to make some judgments on taste. Ideally, we will bend over as far as we can, trying to make sure everyone can offer a product or idea for public consumption.

## The World

Although local news will continue to be more important than other kinds, we cannot duck into our shells and ignore the rest of the world. We have to comment on word news. Weeklies need not hire a correspondent for Europe, but they can have some comment on foreign affairs. If they do it right, they will localize their information—tie it to something in town. (You get more on this topic in Chapter 8, in a reference to localization.)

## Challenge

Newspapers must have aggressive reporting. They must pay reporters a decent wage and then demand that reporters be of top quality. Reporters must do more than go to the council meeting with a garden hose, fill the hose with whatever is said, and then go spray it onto readers. Reporters have to explain. They have to tell how the councilman votes, sure, but they must add some of the why, if they can get it. Legislators are entitled to hold stock in or operate funeral homes, to pick an example, but we readers need to be told about it when they vote on regulation of the business.

A reporter or newspaper should not set out to bring down the government, to destroy labor unions or to rid the country of the lawyer plague. But newspapers must make sure the concentration of power is accountable for the things it does that affect the rest of us. We need not have a knee-jerk reaction that makes us support all underdogs. But we do have to make sure people do not get flattened without good cause.

## Opinion

McCord, who handles opinion pages for the *Gazette,* sees "no reason not to have opinion and commentary in the news columns so long as it is marked with a line that says 'analysis,' 'opinion' or 'commentary'—something like that." He warns against letting grudge carriers settle a score in the newspaper. "If we are going to present opinion and analysis—and we must—then it must be honest opinion and analysis," he says.

## Opinion Page

Every good newspaper must have an opinion section—be it half a page or a 16-page spread. We need to lead, to help the community set its agenda. We need to stir debate, produce thought, and then display that debate and thought for everyone to see. Reader access—letters or guest columns—must be assured. And we ought to run more than one side of a political issue.

## Advantage

McCord likes to tell the story about a midwestern newspaper's Man of the Year contest. The newspaper printed a 16-page special section containing 18 photos of the man and a 5,000-word article. Later, the presentation of the award was the day's lead story, 106 inches long. The Man of the Year was the newspaper's editor and publisher. McCord also complains about glowing book reviews that do not mention that the author is on the news staff, and he worries that newspeople sometimes get obit-page eulogies "that no other citizen, no matter how prominent, could expect."

## Ethics

Ethical problems stay with us always. McCord likes full disclosure—stock ownership by people writing about those stocks; gifts of tickets for people who write about movies or trips abroad. He is also interested in a system for responding to people offended by the news, publication of corrections, and an emphasis on accuracy over speed if the two conflict.

## Friendship

The newspaper should be like a friend invited into a reader's house. You wouldn't want a screamer—someone who constantly preaches catastrophe. You want a friend with a memory, thus providing a flow in the news. You would not want a gossip, or at least not one who puts gossip ahead of honest news. You wouldn't want a friend who constantly emphasizes the negative, who never sees anyone do something right. But you would want a friend who had the ability to set an agenda for your community. Your friend would rank stories for us by importance. He or she would tell us what was important, remembering that we might disagree but causing us to think about our decisions.

Finally, we would want a friend who would help us fight our battles, one who would stand up for us against the unjust.

# Opinion Writing
## We Need More

If it weren't for personal columns, most weekly newspapers would never contain any expression of opinion.

That's too bad. A newspaper cannot make any pretensions to greatness without a strong editorial page.

Oh, I realize most of us have no pretensions to greatness anyway, but that does not mean we can't think about putting out great newspapers. A guy who goes to the shop and says "Well, I guess I'll turn out a mediocre product today" will never make the hall of fame.

Weeklies tend to shy away from editorial pages for a couple of reasons. First, of course, is the matter of space. An editorial page in the *Chicago Tribune* takes up something like 1 percent of the paper, but a page from a weekly takes up 10 to 12 times that percentage. That's a lot of opinion, in my opinion. Second, strong editorial stances tend to produce strong results—not all of them desirable—in small towns. That is, the editor may go to church with the guy he cuts up in an editorial. Or they may eat lunch at adjoining tables at a restaurant. Or, worse, the object of the attack may own the store that does the most advertising with the paper. We're getting too close to home.

Am I encouraging gutlessness? No. But I realize prudence sometimes has a value.

Of course, the editor who is so prudent that he or she would hush something up before offending an advertiser is in the wrong business. Surely editors know when they are remaining silent out of fear of losing an advertiser. And surely that knowledge leaves a hollow spot deep inside.

Fortunately, editors do not face—at least not every day—those life-or-death decisions, the ones in which they either kiss an advertiser's foot or lose the paper. You can't be much of an editor if you don't have a paper, can you? And you aren't much of an editor if you value money over principle, are you?

Nobody said the choices would be easy when you went into the newspaper racket.

Anyway, we started with some thoughts about columns and editorials. Generally, small newspapers are not distinguished by strong editorial pages. They tend to rely on canned material, though most use some local editorials and probably half use a local column. Newspapers in the state I know best, Texas, suffer further from a shortage of community opinion; letters are in short supply and guest columns are rare.

A hint of a cure surfaced at an American Press Institute seminar for 35 editorial-page editors from across the country. These people said unanimously that letters beget more letters. Once readers see that the paper will run letters, they said, readers start writing more letters.

Similarly, people may not ever write guest columns unless they see that the paper uses them. (I refer to long letters that get special treatment as separate articles.) These things operate on the snowball principle, and it is the editor's job to pack the first snow and start it downhill.

Letters and guest columns do not have to take up a whole page. Consequently, even a weekly can give over some space to expressions of opinion in addition to the editor's.

Weekly newspapers almost traditionally run the editor's column on Page 1, and I won't quarrel with that. The column, properly done, ought to have the highest readership of anything in the paper. For one thing, we have a lot good writers in editors' chairs. They are full of opinion, some of it outrageous, some of it wise, most of it interesting. For another thing, columns have a much looser style than news stories, and readers get more deeply involved. Perhaps most important, the editor with any sense will be writing on topics of interest in the community.

Want to know what to write about? Listen to your neighbors talk while drinking coffee before Sunday school or at some other social gathering. People tend to talk about what interests them, so it stands to reason they want to read about it, too. (Let's skip gossip for now.)

OK, how much opinion should an editor express, and how strong should it be?

An editor must be a community leader, but not necessarily the person out front crying "Follow me!" An editor can provide leadership in a column or editorials by giving readers a new way to think about a problem. An editor can be a leader by helping set the community's agenda. That is, an editor brings up things the community needs to consider, and he or she reminds people that problems have not dissolved since they were last discussed.

Editors do not always lead best by writing fire-breathing editorials, the kind that scorch their fellow citizens for small-mindedness. Seldom will a single editorial convert the heathen. It may take you months, or years, of occasional writing about a subject to provide readers with enough information and perspective to come to see the problem as you do.

Buddy Davis, a Pulitzer Prize winner who writes editorials in

Gainesville, Fla., once decided to turn his town around with a piece on school integration. He just about sank the newspaper, because he had not laid any groundwork for the change in policy. Readers were supposed to look at his magic words and have the scales fall from their eyes. Instead, they looked at this surprising turnabout by their newspaper and started hunting their horsewhips. Buddy changed his approach but not his goal. It took time, but he helped get Gainesville integrated.

Now and then, one of your editorials or columns will have the desired effect immediately, and there's some reward in that. Still, you ought not count on a high batting average. Some problems are simply not susceptible to an immediate fix; they require more work.

In the meantime, watch out for those horsewhips.

## Variety

Now we'll look at four kinds of editorials. The terms are artificial, and their use is to give us a vehicle for discussing editorials that you may want to call by some other name. The terminology is not important. Here are the four: Hooray at last. Deer Peepul. Posture. Action.

I got at least two of those from Buddy Davis, mentioned above. He is not responsible for what I do with them.

The hooray-at-last editorial or column is the one in which you let readers know you can say something good about the people and institutions you usually attack. You write these to disarm your adversaries and to bolster your credibility. (You do neither, of course, if you write them without sincerity. I don't mean you should lie your way into the enemy camp.) If you never write anything good about anyone, people get tired of hearing that one tune. But if they think you are fair, that you praise when praise is due, then your criticism gains weight.

The Deer Peepul effort has a place, though seldom will you, or readers, get much of a thrill out of one. This calls for support of the United Fund or the voting campaign or Drive Sober Week. In its worst form, it urges readers to write their congressmen. These can be dull. Write them anyway . . . and try to make them exciting.

Posture editorials do some wonderful things. Sometimes they call for immediate action, but more often they remind people of where you stand and why you believe what you do. The law of expectability comes in here. Readers expect certain things from you, and posture editorials help you tell them what to expect. When you plan an overthrow of the government, or an attack on the pope, or something really drastic, you need to get readers warmed up to the idea. If readers think you believe one thing and all of a sudden find that you're on the other side, they will be surprised and angry—and not as likely to go along with you. So you coax them along, possibly for a matter of years. Give them information and a way to look at it, and you can change opinion. Sometimes.

Action editorials, our fourth category, are probably the most common. They say you want something done. You may be aiming at just one person, maybe more. You could direct your stuff at the movers and shakers, or you could direct it at the masses and hope to get them to pressure the movers and shakers. Either way, you write an editorial with some specific suggestion for immediate action.

While I would never admit to writing by formula or urging others to do so, I want to note three elements that belong in most editorials. A good editorial will have a statement of the problem or situation, some assessment and opinion, and some rationale—your reasons for thinking as you do. These elements can come in any order. You can build up to a climax and then call for action at the end. Or you can start with a cry for the mayor's head and spend the rest of the time explaining why his head should roll. But editorials need those three elements somewhere.

One of the things I like about editorials is that we get such great variety. David Sloan of the University of Alabama put together a book of Pulitzer Prize editorials, and I was enchanted by the variety of styles. Some winners were smooth, urbane, genteel. Others were bombastic, sarcastic, given to slashing their foes unmercifully. (My favorite had a reference to an organization as "a sniveling pus pocket of foot draggers"; we don't write like that anymore.) My basic approach is one of gentility, in the belief that you can catch more flies with honey than you can with vinegar. (OK, so you catch more readers with fresh phrases than with my cliche; sorry.) Also, you do not change a person's opinion by silencing him. Your goal is to look down the road and convert a foe. Get him or her on your side. That's much better than just silencing someone.

It lasts longer, too.

# Help from Outside

Newspapers have never been known for trying to force money on someone who was willing to work for less. So I am puzzled when I see a source of free labor left untouched.

We'll call them guest columnists or guest essayists or guest somethings. Maybe we ought to get a better term than *essayists*. That's a shade fancy for the kind of work I have in mind.

My contention here is that the average town, not just the metropolis, contains people who have something to say and can be persuaded to say it in the columns in your newspaper.

Some subjects come to mind: health, welfare, taxes, education, unemployment, progress, nursing homes, county fairs. And so on. On top of that, some subjects have two clearly opposing sides, and you may get essays on both.

OK, you see trouble in this list. I do, too. You have someone criticizing the local nursing home, and you wind up with a libel suit. Well, editors get paid to referee such things, to guide essayists through the legal briers. You get paid to force these people to stick to charges they can prove. You also get paid to screen out people who have axes to grind and want to use your paper as a whetstone.

Some of the people you would want to do guest columns might more normally be subjects of newspaper interviews. But I see nothing wrong with some duplications there. If you have the president of the chamber of commerce discussing progress in a column, you don't want to ignore a chance to question that person. Let him or her write a column, saying what is likely to happen to the town in the coming year. Follow that with an interview in which you ask the questions the president didn't get around to. Or if you prefer, make suggestions for revisions in the column before you print it.

Let me tell you what brought all this to mind. While looking at some weeklies, I got to wondering why they never had articles on how people in small towns stay fit. You never see a story on exercise. An editor could perform a fine service for a town, even a county, by getting a high school coach to discuss the activities available to all kinds of people. With that as a start, you might goose the school board into letting its facilities be used more in community programs. That, in turn, might bring community members closer together. (Of course, it might cause some fistfights if you had athletic competition and things got spirited, but I won't bring that up now.)

Religion? Well, you might get a column on the state of religion in your town. I don't mean you need a column by the Baptist minister, complaining about the Methodists' being inadequately dipped. I'm thinking more about someone discussing what kinds of things organized religion ought to do in a town.

Or maybe the school board president can write candidly about the quality of your area's schools, including teachers and facilities and the price of improving both.

I don't expect this idea to cause you to be overrun with new-found giants of literature, but I do think you can stir up a little thought, a little discussion and perhaps a little action. And if you fill a column with good stuff at a low price, who's to complain?

# The Letters Column

Newspaper editors sometimes get so busy putting out the paper that they overlook a function that can benefit them and the community.

They slight their place as a forum. I refer specifically to letters to the editor.

Newspapers first provide the news and intelligent comment upon it, of course. But they add a benefit if they get some comment from readers. We don't have much in the way of town meetings anymore, outside of New England, but a letters column can handle some of that role.

One of the drawbacks in a smaller city is that you may stir up more animosity between two readers than you would like. But that's a risk of any kind of public comment. You surely know what it's like to have someone disagree with you on a burning issue.

Besides the philosophical role of being a forum, letters can help create interest in the newspaper. The circulation manager knows what that means. If people look forward to reading the letters for enlightenment or because of the struggle between two sides, that's a plus. No newspaper was ever hurt by having readers eager to see what the next issue had to offer.

So let's assume that we want to run letters. How do we get them? I know this is a problem, because the editor from a California town of 20,000 once told me he got so desperate he salted the mine – he sent himself some letters and published them, in hopes people would catch the habit.

You don't have to go that far, but you do have to accept the basic idea: Print more, get more. If you seldom run letters, people will not be encouraged. If you run an abundance, you stimulate others. Getting started is half the battle. I offer two thoughts, but I suspect you know of others: 1. Call for letters in every edition. Make sure that anyone who visits the editorial office knows you want letters. 2. Offer some bait, perhaps with a topic of the week. For instance, the *Gazette* in Gastonia, N.C., finds a burning issue and asks readers to give their opinions. (The *Gazette* has a telephone line set up for just that purpose, but you can do the same thing by mail.) Then, each Sunday the *Gazette* runs the letters in a page or half-page spread. Looks good. Stirs interest. Stirs thought. Probably stirs circulation.

After you get letters flowing, you need some method of display. A lot of papers use a full column of letters down the right side of the editorial page. Consistency is the key there. Readers of those newspapers know where to find letters. You can group them other ways—across the bottom, boxed in 2, 3 or 4 columns, whatever you want. But you do need to make them stand out a bit so readers will know you put some value on them. You have a lot of choices on salutation (*Dear Editor, To the Editor, Editor,* nothing) and individual headlines. Use what you like. Look at exchange papers for ideas. Experiment.

A letters column is not an unalloyed blessing. Somebody has to look after them and make sure you have them all. You have to worry about fake letters; that means you have to verify all letters, or at least the ones that raise any kind of stink. You have to decide what to do about anonymous letters. Most papers, I am told, do not use anonymous letters. Some make exception for someone, such as a policeman's wife in one case, who might be subject to abnormal reaction. Generally, the rule is that the writer needs to be able to stand the heat if he or she wants to get into a controversy.

You need to consider, too, what you do if a writer attacks someone. Do you tell the attacked person ahead of time and allow for a response in the same issue? Most papers that answered a survey I saw did that, except for public figures. That is, a letter might attack the mayor without warning, because the mayor expects criticism and knows how to reply. The mayor has access to channels of communication—he or she can call a news conference or make a statement and know that it will get into the paper. An ordinary citizen, on the other hand, may not know how to get his case before the public, having been brought into a controversy only once.

Finally, you need some policy on ending controversy. That has to be an editorial decision. You have to decide when a controversy has run its course. You have have to decide, too, how many letters you want to print on a given topic. If you get 20 similar letters (not a blitz by a group, just 20 letters on the same subject), you may want to run the best 3 or 4 and list the names of other people who wrote on that subject.

No matter how you do it, your newspaper will benefit if you are able to get a lively letters column. You can't start from zero and pull this off overnight. But you can't do it at all if you don't start now.

# Reviews

Let's see whether we can decide how big a newspaper should be before it does local reviews on books, movies and theater.

One of the newspapers I read quit doing local movie reviews a while ago. The editor reasoned this way:

1. The city, despite a population of 250,000, is not a film center; movies open in other places first.
2. The newspaper cannot justify the expense of a full-time person, and a part-timer would mean that quality was below standard.
3. Wires and syndicates can provide material by more knowledgeable people. Those people have more time to go where movies are made, talk to stars and filmmakers and generally immerse themselves in that business.
4. Movie material will be screened and reviewed earlier by outside sources—they either attend openings or get previews, long before the material gets to this city.

You can see some logic in all those ideas.

Perhaps we can find logic on the flip side.

If you have local reviews, your readers get a report on a movie as seen by a person whose views more nearly resemble those of readers than do the views of a New Yorker or a Hollywood chap—assuming your reviewer has not just moved to town. For instance, a reviewer in Odessa, Texas, might be thrilled by a scene showing rain, whereas a fellow from Baton Rouge, La., wouldn't make much of it.

Then, too, experts sometimes get carried away. They come forth with much wind and go insane over some weird director's new technique. They tell us a lot more about movies than we really want to know. They get too busy being experts and forget to be reporters. Maybe all we readers want is a report on whether we would like the movie.

In addition, the local reviewer will be able to give a reader some perspective. He or she will presumably know how similar movies have been treated in the past in the city—whether anyone went to see them. And the local reviewer will be able to phone theater owners if a review requires something special. (Nothing comes to mind. I mainly mean that last statement in a negative way: Wire service reviewers aren't going to check on the local scene.)

Finally, we have to talk about money. We do save by using wire and syndicate people. But if we decide that the local touch is not worth the expense, do we then clean out the Capitol bureaus and let AP give us all the coverage we need from the statehouse? Perhaps that's another subject.

Can we have this both ways? I would like to think so. I would like to think we get the expertise of full-time people who work where movies are made and not give up the local touch. If I were editor in the city under discussion, I would be content to use outside material on most movies. But I would certainly encourage local work on some things—the big movies and anything with local connections.

I would encourage the entertainment editor to give movies full coverage, for they do make a contribution to the life of a lot of people.

The same goes for the theater and books. I would find a staffer with an interest in theater or, depending on the city, would enlist the help of a teacher or other knowledgeable person to handle theater coverage. Above all, that sort of effort needs mention in the newspaper.

As for books, I would probably use the system once in effect at the *Denton Record-Chronicle.* There, Ray Stephens, a history teacher at North Texas State, got all the books and placed them with people who knew something about the subject matter. He built up a stable of reviewers who gave a local look at new offerings. Most came from the faculties of two universities in town. Supplement those with wire and syndicate reviews from New York and you are in business. (Actually, Ray is no longer in the business. He got to be mayor and started reading financial reports and such things.)

To summarize: Get as much local input as you can without disrupting your budget and without making your reviewers go beyond their ability.

# 12

# Ethical Matters

Setting standards ● Sensitivity ● More on ethics ● *Why people dislike the media. The SPJ ethics report.* Ads in disguise ● *Goodbye, credibility. Who writes those things?*

## Setting Standards

Someone asked me about journalism ethics the other day, and I had to say I had none. Or at least I have none that I would try to foist off on someone else. No one should try such foisting. Your ethical standards start with you, and they are highly personal.

They do come up for discussion now and then, and we cannot ignore the topic. Newspaper publishers have the right—let's call it an obligation—to set up policies covering ethical matters.

Those policies tell reporters and others where to draw lines to keep from hurting the newspaper. If an employee wants to make his or her own standards even tighter than those of the newspaper, no one should quarrel with that view. If an employee's personal ethics conflict with the publisher's on every point, perhaps another line of work would be more fitting.

Ethics come in two categories for newspeople: how we gather information, and what we do with it.

The arrogance that Americans attribute to the press rises largely from our actions in gathering news. We seek and accept—and sometimes buy— secret records from grand juries, investigating panels and others. We peek at memos on desks, and some of us pry into files if we get a chance. We go undercover to spy on some miscreant, but we get apoplectic if the FBI infiltrates some group of citizens, even terrorists.

Generally, we do those things because we believe newspeople all have pure motives, while we are suspicious of the FBI's. Unfortunately, the public does not accept the purity of our hearts as readily as we do. The public believes we will do anything to get a story that will sell newspapers, no matter what harm it does to the nation.

Indeed, our disregard of the right of privacy is one of the areas that draws strong criticism. Is the public hypocritical? Yes. People criticize you for you running a story about a grieving mother, but such stories draw readers.

# Sensitivity

The most vital part of your ethical makeup is sensitivity.

Mike Royko, in one of his last columns before leaving the *Chicago Sun-Times,* told about a baseball player named Lennie Murello. Lennie was like Marv Thornberry of the Mets, except that he didn't do beer commercials. He batted .245 for the Cubs and usually led the league in errors while Royko was growing up. Royko often used Lennie in a humorous annual column about the Cubs. Lennie was the butt of jokes.

One day Lennie wrote. He told the columnist about his four wonderful grown sons and his wife of 45 years and his grandchildren. He told about his job, as a respected baseball scout. He admitted he had not been a star, but he said he had tried – maybe too hard.

More followed, all in a gentle tone. And at the end Lennie had reminded Mike Royko that all those incompetent athletes we assail, all those politicians we ridicule, all those people whose grief we expose to our readers – all those newsmakers are humans, like us.

Keeping that in mind will not keep us from doing our jobs; we can still comfort the afflicted and afflict the comfortable. But we just might do the job a little better.

# More on Ethics
## Why People Dislike the Media

Now I want to emphasize things we do that readers dislike and for which they distrust us. Not all involve ethics, but I will give you the list anyway. This list comes from a splendid ethics roundup prepared by the Society of Professional Journalists. The organization prepares an annual report in tabloid newspaper form.

People say they dislike these press traits: inaccuracy, arrogance, unfairness, disregard of privacy, insensitivity, contempt for local ways, and glorification of bizarre or criminal acts.

## INACCURACY

Ah, we're vulnerable. Our work gives us a terrific variety of ways to make errors, and some of us try every way. We can defend judgment calls and can dispute taste and such things, but we cannot wipe out the stain of inaccuracy. All we can do is redouble our efforts to get everything right.

## ARROGANCE

We take the position that inasmuch as our hearts are pure, we have privileges others do not. I think we do. But we abuse our privileges at times—and never admit guilt.

## UNFAIRNESS

We do not make an adequate effort to demonstrate our fairness. We write one-sided stories with only a perfunctory effort to get the other side. We let ourselves be used by people with an ax to grind.

## DISREGARD OF PRIVACY

Some people are thrown into the news through no fault of their own, and they come out sorely bruised. I do not know how to eliminate this problem and still tell readers what happens around them. A victim of crime, or that victim's relatives, or the criminal's relatives will be thrust into the spotlight's glare quickly. We run into ethical considerations when we make a decision on the use of a photo of a grieving mother, for example. Our dilemma is that people criticize us for running such photos but indicate by their readership that they will look at them.

## INSENSITIVITY

This one has obvious links to privacy. Perhaps we ought to have newsroom discussions of sensitivity. The easiest test I can think of involves asking whether you would want yourself or a relative to be portrayed as you portray others. *Want* is the wrong word. No one wants to be involved in sad news. The question is whether you think such treatment is *proper* for you as well as for those other people.

CONTEMPT FOR LOCAL WAYS

This complaint occurs more often when an out-of-town organization owns the paper than when a local family does. It means the newspaper should be seen as a part of the community, not as a judge removed from the scene. You do not have to be a booster in the sense that you ignore blemishes, but you have to be perceived as someone who enjoys living where you live.

GLORIFICATION OF BIZARRE OR CRIMINAL ACTS

This answer popped up, I suspect, because people felt that newspapers often seem to take the side of a person fighting valiantly to avoid execution. We forget the deed that landed the killer on death row in the first place. As for the bizarre, I saw one front-page story about a man and a woman who tied themselves together for a year — eight feet of rope between them — and called the act "performance art."

Those general topics described above cause us problems in the public mind. We are seen as imperfect there. And we probably are. A person could develop each of those topics into a day's discussion and probably not solve anything.

Does that mean we should not mess with discussions of ethics? Does it mean we leave ethics up to the individual?

Yes and no. No one can force you to be ethical by his or her standards. I would like to cause you to think about these things, think about the way you do your job. Let me quote from the ethics report cited in the second paragraph: "Like everyone else, journalists do not live in black and white purity, but rather with blurred relationships and shades of gray. Only by talking about this and wrestling with it openly can we create an atmosphere in which the lines not to cross will be clearly marked."

## The SPJ Ethics Report

You are behind in your reading if you have not finished the ethics report and freedom of information report from the Society of Professional Journalists. Great stuff.

The society puts out tabloid sections on freedom of information and on ethics. These have caused me to do some shuffling near the end of the semester and add three hours on ethics to a journalism class I teach. I have always had something on ethics in every class, but the SPJ tabs convinced me more was necessary.

You will be convinced, too — convinced the people at your publication need to spend a bit of time in discussing ethics. If you want a copy of the report as a guide, write SPJ/SDX, 53 W. Jackson Blvd., Suite 731, Chicago, Ill. 60604-3610. Ask for the ethics and FOI reports. I would send a dollar or two, or more, for handling, but that's just because I am so ethical.

Or maybe I'm not. My answers did not always jibe with those of people questioned in a national survey SPJ did to prepare one year's report. However, none of the questions got unanimous responses. People see different things different ways.

This does not mean that ethics cannot be cultivated. The lack of unanimity does not mean that we should ignore the subject. Indeed, we have to discuss these things. We have to turn them over in our minds until we get some kind of inner understanding. A publisher can impose a code of ethics from without, and I think publishers should, but true ethics come from within. You have ethics because you know the difference between right and wrong. We all know the difference, but sometimes we get in too much of a hurry to think about it.

The SPJ reports can help you overcome that shortcoming. They touch a lot of bases. One had a strong section on plagiarism. This column plagiarizes that report liberally.

One year's report had a great section on deception. The writer looked at four degrees of deception: primary lack of identification, passive misrepresentation, active misrepresentation, and masquerading.

In the first, lack of identification, journalists might check on apartments without identifying themselves, for example. They could find out whether apartments were available. But they would be obliged to say they were reporters when they started asking questions about how rents were determined or why children were not allowed.

The next step up the ladder of deception, passive misrepresentation, would occur, for example, at a public meeting at which a reporter acted like a member of the general public, and the person being questioned did not realize he or she was talking for publication. Say a group of women at a public meeting talked about being victims of sexual crimes. They would not talk as freely if they knew a reporter was present; thus the flow of information would be inhibited. (You can argue this sort of thing, of course. The women should be encouraged to talk for the media so that thousands of people instead of dozens could benefit from their knowledge. Getting them to talk requires some sensitivity from reporters.)

The report gives as an example of active misrepresentation a case in which a reporter told parents she was doing a story on the tragedy of a teenager's suicide. The reporter wrote a piece about how the parents' attitudes had contributed to that suicide. They had no chance to respond to that hypothesis.

That gets us to masquerading. Take the case of the *Wilmington* (N.C.) *Morning Star,* whose reporters infiltrated nearby Camp Lejeune soon after 270 Marines were killed by a bomb in Beirut. Reporters drove right into the camp in trucks that could have carried explosives. One came in the back way by boat and got into the camp commander's home by asking to use the bathroom. They exposed a woeful lack of security.

Should they have?

Why don't you discuss that with the staff? Why don't you get the SPJ reports and discuss their ramifications? These things come up every day, in some guise or other, and the way we handle them affects our credibility. That's worth a little time, wouldn't you say?

# Ads in Disguise
## Goodbye, Credibility

Some newspapers run ads that look like news stories. They ought to consider a change of policy.

I do not want to sound moralistic, because we are discussing someone else's money, not mine. Nevertheless, I want to encourage you to avoid giving anyone the idea that news columns are for sale. You know they aren't for sale. I know they aren't for sale. But the public does not always realize the breadth of our virtue. People sometimes assume they can get a story in the paper if they pay for it. We need to disabuse them of that notion.

Newspapers run advertiser-written stories that require either direct payment for running the story as an ad, or indirect payment by buying an ad, for which the story is run as an ordinary news story. These are commonly called reader ads.

I do not know of a newspaper that would present a reader ad without some sort of caveat. Newspapers usually put them on special pages, and they offer some clear notation – well, sort of clear – that the stories are ads instead of news stories, despite the appearance.

One of the papers I read runs this kind of material in a section prominently labeled Advertiser CLOSE-UP. A smaller line says this is an advertising supplement. No problem there. Some of the stories have color art, and they all carry headlines in Lydian, a typeface different from the paper's normal headline face. (By itself, a change in headline face is not enough. Regular readers do not pay much attention to type.)

Another newspaper has a standing headline on its Business and Industrial Directory, including a line saying, "All items on this page are paid advertising." And one has a similar line in the page logo: "This page produced by the display advertising department."

The *Northwest Florida Daily News* in Fort Walton Beach used to run a full page of reader ads each Monday. It used a typeface markedly different from the regular head dress and had big body type set three columns wide and in a fashion that clearly distinguished it from the regular material. A line in the page logo (Business Review) said, "Reader ads in this section prepared by Contract Advertising, Inc." I like this style. No normal reader would confuse the ads with news stories.

An Ohio newspaper has a Page 3 column called News Flashes and Announcements. It contains a few news paragraphs – such as meeting times for the school board and maybe a death notice or two. It has a lot more ads, an inch or so long, all written in news style. These are low-budget ads, and the amateur ad writers go for all-cap wording. Most ads are thus easily detected. However, a few look no different from the regular news blurbs.

Something similar appears in a California newspaper, with a column called News and Briefs. The heading gives no indication that the column contains both sheep and goats. However, the word *adv.* appears at the end of each ad, taking some of the sting off my objection there. Still, ads and news switch back and forth, and readers have to pay attention or be fooled.

This mingling of ads and news runs the risk of having people think the news columns are for sale. I wouldn't mingle them. If for some reason they absolutely have to be mingled, ads should have a different format to distinguish them from news.

Are advertisers ashamed to admit they run ads? Of course not. But they object to our use of an *adv.* label on reader ads because they want readers to think the ad's information is as unbiased as your newspaper. They want people to think you looked at the subject objectively and wrote those nice things just as you would have if you had investigated a politician or toxic waste dump or other maker of news.

I apologize for not knowing much about the other side of this controversy, if it is a controversy. What possibilities do we have for the other side, the non-news side? Well, ads bring in money, and we need money to operate. I have no quarrel with the profit motive. However, we can sell ads without selling souls, too. We can put advertising in the regular places and in regular formats; the loss of reader ads should not be crucial.

Some publishers, in supporting the other side, will say readers are sophisticated enough to see the difference. I wish that were true. I guess a quarter of your readers think they can buy their way into your pages, largely because they see reader ads.

## Who Writes Those Things?

One other aspect: Who should prepare reader ads? The news staff ought to be kept as far from them as possible. You should not have a reporter write a story that tells about a company being cited for illegally fouling the atmosphere, for example, and then get the reporter to do a reader ad telling us what a wonderful company this is. Even worse would be to do a story about something good the company has done and then do a reader ad. A reporter who takes money to write good things—the reader ad—about a company or store will one day have trouble convincing people he or she didn't take money to write something good—the news—the next day. Readers can't understand, and can't believe, the quick change of hats. Ad people should be paid to prepare ads. Newspeople should be paid to prepare news. I can accept the practice of having the news side put out a special section on, say, gardening, as long as we have honest news and features as opposed to stories written only to glorify a product.

We need to do more to build credibility, not whittle away at it.

I worry that this advice is impractical for small weeklies. Some do not have enough employees to separate ad sellers from news gatherers. I think I would pretend if I ran a small weekly. I would pretend to be two people, selling ads sometimes and getting the news sometimes. I would not let the two overlap.

That bit of silliness would not hold up long, I suspect, but I would try. Anything would be better than trying to write a story about someone when his ad is on your mind. You will never convince readers that you don't consider the ad when you write about the person.

# 13

## Let's Do Better Work

Self-help I: a list of books • Self-help II: staff improvement
program • Self-help III: critiques • Helping
stringers • Look around • Contests I: what they
offer • Contests II: judging yourself

## Self-Help I: A List of Books

You cannot become a good writer just by reading about writing. But that does not mean you should ignore the many good books about writing. You have chosen to make a living with words, and anything you can do to strengthen your ability to use them should be worthwhile.

Books will offer some information, of course, but their main value comes in focusing your attention upon your craft. Books remind you to look hard at your own work. Some people never get the habit of examining their work. Without examining it, they cannot improve it. A pity.

Every writer should regularly spend time going over his or her work and reading what others have to say about the language.

If I were a newspaper publisher and wanted to encourage newsroom employees to improve their writing, I would break out the cashbox and see that my people had access to books about writing. I would start with *When Words Collide*, by Lauren Kessler and Duncan McDonald (Wadsworth Publishing Co., Belmont, Calif.). This book does as much as any to simplify the intricacies of writing. It has both the basics (such as the difference between a gerund and a verb) and the advanced stuff (how to write with style).

In addition to the general reference works—dictionary, thesaurus, and so on—I would have Prentice-Hall's *Handbook for Writers* on the shelf. Splendid basic English work. Prentice-Hall, which publishes a number of books about our field, is in Englewood Cliffs, N.J.

In your letter to Prentice-Hall, you may also want to ask for *Writing With Style,* by John Trimble. John doesn't say much about principles and those things, but he sure shows you some ways to improve your work.

Prentice-Hall also published Ken Metzler's *Creative Interviewing.* Newspaper people ought to have that book on the shelf—after a thorough reading. It's not about language, but it's still valuable.

Certainly our list must include *The Elements of Style,* by William Strunk Jr. and E.B. White (Macmillan, 866 Third Ave., New York, N.Y. 10022). This little paperback is full of good advice.

James J. Kilpatrick came out with *The Writer's Art* for one Christmas season, and that made a great present from Santa. Kilpatrick pads the book with a dictionary section dealing with troublesome words, but he can be forgiven. Others do the dictionary work better, but few offer more solid thoughts about writing in general. Andrews, McMeel & Parker (4400 Johnson Dr., Fairway, Kan. 66205) published the book.

Put Roy Copperud on your list of people with the dictionary approach. His *Dictionary of Usage* (Hawthorn Publishers, New York) is perhaps the best in that line.

Theodore Bernstein, late assistant managing editor of the *New York Times,* has dictionary elements in his last book, *The Careful Writer* (Atheneum, New York). He went beyond that, however, and gave us a fine book, the last before his death. His earlier books also had good advice.

Say good things about John Bremner, whose *Words on Words* was published by Columbia University Press, New York. John, a former Jesuit scholar and priest from Australia, taught journalism well at the University of Kansas and then traveled extensively for the Gannett Company. His book entertains as well as enlightens. Sometimes he gives you more enlightenment (as a person who speaks Greek and Latin might) than you truly need. But he always entertains. He died in 1987, but his work lives on.

Edwin Newman, the TV fellow, did two decent books on language. He has a fine talent for spotting high-flown bureaucratic language and turning it into something the rest of us can grasp. The books, *Strictly Speaking* and *A Civil Tongue,* were merged into one paperback, available from Bobbs-Merril Co., 4300 W. 62nd St., Indianapolis, Ind.

William Saffire, like Kilpatrick a political columnist who does a weekly piece on the language, has turned some of his material into a book, *On Language* (New York Times Books). You will enjoy this one, but don't buy it until you have read most of the others mentioned here.

William Zinsser's *On Writing Well* has been widely praised — more than it deserves. However, you ought to look into it, just to see if you disagree with any of it. It has some good parts.

Some of the fun of reading books like these comes from the arguing. For instance, Kilpatrick contends that you ought not separate the parts of a verb with an adverb in most cases. Kilpatrick would change the sentence *He had consistently opposed capital punishment* to *He had opposed capital punishment consistently.* He's wrong in insisting on the change, and he's wrong in criticizing Fowler for an opposing view.

Did someone mention Fowler? That's the sainted H.W. Fowler, whose *Modern English Usage* (Oxford University Press, London) set the standard. I treasure my Fowler above all the others. You probably can't find a copy, but you will have a gem if you do.

You can settle for some of these others without disappointment. Happy reading.

# Self-Help II: Staff Improvement Program

Most newspaper people have little to do and consequently rush to embrace suggestions that require more work.

I expect to be overwhelmed with gratitude for the following suggestions. They tell you how to go about a staff improvement program. I address this to newsroom supervisors, but it could be for those they designate to do the job. Not every news editor or managing editor has the time and background to do this sort of thing. Reporters, copy editors and other bright creatures will find the material pertinent, too. I hope.

First, be systematic. Sit down with a reporter for half an hour after work one or two days a week. Rotate the reporters systematically. Before the meeting, examine that person's copy thoroughly. You have to be prepared. No shortcuts.

Then you go over the person's copy with the writer or editor.

You do not have to cover every sentence the reporter wrote since the last meeting. You will be all right if you cover problems that crop up repeatedly.

While you have the reporter's ear, go over someone else's good work (not a staffer's) and see whether you two can agree on what makes it different.

This approach will remind the staff you want a better newspaper. It will show them you will spend your energy to get it.

You need to take the collective approach, too. Do a roundup of good and bad things you see in your newspaper. Name the good guys. Let the others be anonymous, because you should attack the sin, not the sinner.

If you do not have time or inclination for this work, get someone outside to help. Get the job done right, and without harshness. Your goal is to get people interested in improving their work, not in making them afraid to touch the VDT keys.

A friend of mine from California works this another way. He rotates the critics. A different staffer marks up the paper each week. All have started reading the newspaper a little more closely.

Enter contests. Oh, you may want to skip those that require you to write something favorable about some subject. (Rules do not specify that, but you know how things work.) Go for most contests. See how you measure up against your peers. You may win honor and respect and, sometimes, money. Bear in mind that the judging will be subjective. Your splendid entry may finish behind someone else's mediocre offering. Don't let that bother you; learn from the experience. And remember that the main judge is the person who gets your newspaper. Think of readers before judges. You will find more on this subject at the end of this chapter.

Attack errors. Send clippings to four or five people whose names appear in your stories. Ask about accuracy of the stories. Ask about fairness. Ask about the headline. Ask what the reader would like to see in your newspaper. Send a stamped envelope.

Encourage staff reading. The newsroom should have an abundance of books about this business. Buy some for the desk. Get them out there where people can get at them; if one gets stolen, it will still do more good than it would do hidden away in a private office.

What kind of books? Some on writing are cited in this chapter. You might also try books on photos, such as *Pictures on a Page,* by Harold Evans. Try books on layout. Try them all.

Mainly, you must encourage people. Our staffers do not get to be better by accident. They learn by reading. They learn by examining their own material carefully, critically. They learn by talking with editors and peers. They learn by sharing.

Newspaper people are in the business of working with words and pictures. It seems to me they would spend as much time as possible in improving their tools.

# Self-Help III: Critiques

A young graduate of the institution that keeps me out of the breadlines wrote for advice. She had been with a newspaper in Missouri for a couple of years, and she had become dissatisfied with her professional growth.

She got no help from her bosses, who railroaded her copy into the paper just about the way she wrote it. She was wise enough to realize that her material had an occasional flaw. What to do?

I gave her three alternatives: 1. Bundle up her clips and look for a job on a better-edited publication. 2. Go back to school for a year simply to acquire more skills in journalism or some other field, some specialty, if she had the money. 3. Sit down with the boss and help him realize he or his deputies ought to help her and the rest of the newsroom improve.

I favor the third choice, which may cause a revolution in her newsroom. More newsrooms need such a revolution.

Ah, but I can hear the roar of editors now, saying they aren't running a school, saying Gibson should not have let an uneducated reporter get out of his school in the first place.

Horsefeathers. Colleges are supposed to turn out people with a thorough grounding in the basics of journalism, people able to cover events and write understandable stories quickly. We let some turkeys get through now and then, and I apologize for that. But not even the good ones will be polished reporters from day one. The people who win Pulitzer Prizes do not work for $229.40 a week. (I use that figure because it is the beginning rate for garbage collectors where I live. Surely we pay as much to dish it out as the city does to collect it.)

Some things come only with experience, and even experience carries no guarantee. The good editor will make sure that young reporters and editors benefit as much as possible from the experience of their elders. They—make that *you*—do not have to set up a formal class, but you really do need to provide regular feedback to all your people. You need to find some way to help newcomers over hurdles that you had to struggle with. I don't mean editors should be nursemaids, but they should help newcomers improve.

If the *New York Times* finds it necessary to provide a running critique of the work of its $800-a-week reporters, handled by $900-a-week copy editors, surely other papers can find something worthwhile in the idea.

A monthly review of the good and bad things you have done — from subject matter of stories to fine points of writing and layout and headlines and photos and so on — should be beneficial in three main ways:

1. It should reward good performance with recognition.
2. It should point out and help eliminate recurring errors.
3. It should cause us all to do our work a little better, cause us to look at a sentence carefully enough to see any lack of clarity — and rewrite it. Similarly, it should cause us to go after better photographs or redo layout to get rid of awkwardness.

Most newspapers are likely to have someone able to do this critique work tactfully, but those people normally have other chores that take up most of their time. This kind of work is time-consuming, I assure you.

Now, this next part is not an ad, because I have more work now than I can say grace over, especially when we consider that the Legislature wants me to work for my little salary. However, if you know a journalism teacher or retired newsperson or perhaps you have a friend on another newspaper — someone somewhere whose judgment you respect — you might arrange for an outside critique. An outsider's fresh viewpoint can sometimes be of great value, even if you disagree with everything the outsider says.

Anything that gets us out of ruts, especially ruts we did not realize we were in, is likely to be worth the cost.

# Helping Stringers

My intention in this book has generally been to try to unlock the secrets of the universe. I refer to the lesser secrets, not the biggies such as who shot J.R.

This time we take a look at correspondents, who are called stringers in newspaper parlance. I will deal with some of their shortcomings, as reflected in the pages of your newspapers.

By far the most common problem I run across in the writing of correspondents is the use of the chronology approach on meeting stories. Maybe you call it the minutes approach – in which the story reads like the minutes of the meeting. It smells bad under either name.

I recall one such offering that told who called the meeting to order, who presided (the president), who gave the invocation and what was on the menu, taking up the first 80 percent of the story. The final paragraph mentioned that the group had chosen new officers.

You don't have to be a foreign correspondent for the *Manchester Guardian* to understand how far off that lead was. I realize the rural countryside is not overrun with Pulitzer Prize winners eager to supplement their income by stringing for a newspaper. Still, the editor is responsible for the quality of all copy that goes into the paper, and he or she ought to do better.

Some of us, because of the lack of time or because we are afraid we will lose a stringer if we offer criticism or because of Lord knows what else, just funnel this stuff right on in. That's not fair to readers. Readers expect more, or at least would respect more. It's not really fair to the correspondents, either. They can't get better unless they realize they need to improve.

I have heard readers laugh off an obvious error and say, "Oh, it's just our little hometown newspaper." How patronizing can they get? If you are a married male, try saying to your to your wife some morning after breakfast, "Those biscuits weren't very good this morning, but they are about as good as I could expect from you, I guess." (Don't try this unless you have a good cafe in your town or you plan to begin a fast.) That's the same attitude the newspaper patronizers have, and it ought to rankle you.

I realize, of course, that many editors would rather use inferior copy than go through the hassle required to get top-quality material. Perhaps it would be easier on you in the long run if you forced correspondents to do their work the way you really want it, even at the risk of losing one. You wouldn't have to keep looking at such junky copy.

That may be the wrong approach. But other approaches must have flaws, or they wouldn't produce what we have.

# Look Around

A couple of stories you didn't see provide lessons for the willing observer. You didn't see them because they had no national prominence. Nor should they have had any. But they contained something worth considering.

One told of a young man's bus ride to his new job. Most of us, I suspect, do not give Trailways and Greyhound much business these days. We have cut ourselves off from the segment of society that rides the bus. (I don't want to make that a total putdown. My sister, who has a fancy car, rides the bus 300 miles to the big city if she doesn't want to drive and airline connections require long layovers.)

But this young reporter rode from Fort Worth to Pampa. He kept his eyes open. He talked. He listened. He learned something about people. We all know the country has people who have problems. We generally go out of our way to avoid them. Our reporter didn't, and he's a better man for the experience. We should all have so much courage.

Better than that, we should all have enough sense to expose ourselves to something we do not normally see. Our newspapers would improve.

The other story grew from an encounter in a laundromat. A reporter in Greenville, Miss., found a man sleeping on a table there. He struck up a conversation, as reporters sometimes do. The sleeper was out of work, hungry and broke, and he would have been far from home if he had had a home.

After feeding him, the reporter asked why social agencies— Salvation Army, Red Cross—had not helped. No scandal. The fellow had just fallen through the cracks. He had gone to the right places at the wrong times. The reporter learned that Greenville's soup kitchens don't operate on the weekends, but the policy was re-evaluated because of the reporter.

Now for the lesson: This reporter focused on one person, one homeless, poor person, as a microcosm of a problem for the city. He did a much better job in making us see what it's like to be poor than if he had thrown statistics at us.

We read about a million people getting killed in a typhoon in Bangladesh, or about 10,000 dying in an earthquake in Mexico, and we're sorry. The mind comprehends these facts. But it's not until we get down to individual suffering that the heart understands. It's not until we start pulling for one kid trapped under debris that we get our most human feelings.

Some of you will remember Kathy Fiscus, a child who was trapped in a well four decades ago. She captured everyone's attention for days before she died. (Some of you will remember Floyd Collins, trapped in a cave, but that's too far back for most of us.) These were real people, caught in danger. We knew them. We grieved at their deaths. We would have exulted in their rescue.

So let me recap the wisdom we should steal from two young reporters. First, all of us need to spend a little more time with people who are our peers in humanity if not in fiscal solvency. I'm not talking about sleeping on Skid Row. I mean you ought to spend a day on a garbage truck or a day on a farmer's tractor or a day in a nursing home. You—and I and most others in this business—need to know more about the people who live around us. We can't learn it by sitting in the office.

Second, you need to remember to focus on individuals when writing about cosmic subjects. When you write about eliminating welfare programs, have in mind someone who will be affected. (Hold it. Watch out for the knee jerks. I may be asking you to think of some young mother who won't have money to feed her baby, or I may be asking you to think of some lazy loafer who doesn't work because he can feed at the public trough just as easily.)

Do these things and you will be closer to your community. If you don't do them, who will? You get paid to tell me what goes on in the community. To tell, you must first learn.

# Contests I: What They Offer

Earl Luedcke and I once worked together in judging a state press association contest. After all the work was done, we met in the hospitality room at a convention and discussed our handiwork.

I asked Earl why he didn't enter the contest, since he puts out a newspaper as good as any its size.

Let me say right off that I disagree with Earl's view here, though I understand it. His idea, and it makes some sense, is that he puts out the *News* for the people in his area (Sealy, Texas) and thus has a contest every week. If the people like what he's doing and indicate that warmth by supporting his newspaper, he has done what he wanted to do.

Well said. Earl is indeed looking at the ultimate contest. Community support is first prize, second prize and the only real prize.

However, contests have other functions, and we might benefit from some examination of them.

First, contests generally enable you to see a concentration of the best work of your peers, especially if winners are displayed at a convention. You could see the same thing by going through all your exchange papers, but in a contest someone else—the editors and judges—does the culling for you.

Second, you may get to have someone else toot your horn for you and say kind words about you. Most of us are able to bear up under that sort of treatment. It's nice to know your peers recognize the quality of your work.

Third, and here we have the most valuable part of competition, you may improve your work because you concentrate a little more. You may get sharper under constant reminders that the payoff for perfection is greater than that for mediocrity. You may be encouraged to go back over a story and sharpen a lead or lift an adequate headline to the zinger level. Or you may be inspired to enhance a good photo with imaginative cropping and display.

If you do these things, you will surely not lessen your community support. You may even increase it.

Contests have their negative aspects, of course. Nobody likes to be told that his or her scintillating series on school bonds or the hospital or the water district was not as good as somebody else's flimsy little piece on drugs or drag racing or whatever. That hurts.

Then, too, judges may err, or at least differ. All editors can cite examples in which a newspaper won a second place somewhere with an entry that won some other contest. I know of a newspaper that was judged best student paper in a two-state region by the Society of Professional Journalists—one week after it finished third at another respected contest, with about the same competition. These things happen, especially when you have a number of high-class entries.

All in all, though, the advantages of entering contests outweigh the disadvantages. Contests can help you put out a better newspaper. They can help you see how someone else looks at your paper, right or wrong.

Newspaper contests are not like football games, in which one team wins and the other loses. In newspaper contests, judges say one entry is good, and the other, far from being a loser, is just a non-winner.

Some people take home ribbons and plaques and certificates from contests. We call those people winners. Do you know what we call those others, those who do not gather an armload of contest loot? I don't know what word you use, but I call most of them winners, too.

# Contests II: Judging Yourself

Newspaper contests have a lot in common with the crooked roulette wheel: They have drawbacks, but they're the only game in town.

Or at least they offer something you can't get elsewhere.

They offer these things: Recognition by your peers. An assessment by an outsider. Marketable glory—they make your newspaper a little more valuable when you win.

Drawbacks come mainly in the judging. Most people who enter contests firmly believe the judging was handled by semiliterate incompetents. You find a few newspeople who do not think this. These people won the contests.

Perhaps I exaggerate. You do not hear harsh criticism of judging from newspapers. Now and then editors will admit they thought the winning entry was no better than their own, but most aren't nasty about it.

Besides, that brings us to a major point in any discussion of worthiness: You have to do your own judging of yourself and of others. You have to look at your entry and judge it against the winner. You do not have to agree the winner was better, for subjectivity comes into play strongly in any judging. You need only look at your entry more carefully. Examine its flaws, if any are noted by the judge. Decide whether your work is better than the winner's. If it is, congratulate yourself. Don't let your bad luck in the contest gnaw on you. Just try to see things through the judge's eyes.

Now, about those judges. Some state associations trade judging with other states on occasion. That has become a popular method of getting the job done. You get judged by peers that way. Universities sometimes supply judges. Or entries can be spread among individual newspapers and staffers. That is, you might get someone in Baltimore to judge news and someone in Chicago to do photos. The Headliners Club in Austin does its statewide contest that way, picking people who have no connection to any chain that has a Texas newspaper. (Finding such people is a trick in itself. Entries are screened, and no judge gets more than 10; that makes the judging task fairly simple.)

No matter how the judging is done, you need to help yourself win by properly packaging your entry after you carefully select it.

Let me tell you some of the things that go through a judge's mind.

In newswriting and feature writing, judges are turned off by an awkward lead or, even worse, one with a grammatical mistake. A good lead gives you a leg up in any contest. Most judges make a fairly quick pass through the entries first, setting aside say half of them to read again. On the second pass, they read more thoroughly. A good lead will probably get you into the second round, though not always. A stinker of a lead will probably cause the judge to pass you by, though, again, not always. It will give you a handicap that must be overcome by some strong writing.

The handling of photo and layout entries is similar to that of stories. A great photo, run 2-by-4 with murky reproduction, will not win prizes consistently. Judges are human, and they will be more favorably impressed by a big photo that jumps out at them in detail than by a dark midget. They look for good composition and framing and even imagination, but they won't squint to do it. Also, good layout printed poorly will not be honored. And good headline ideas cannot carry a headline that has a grammatical lapse or typo.

How about your packaging of the entry? Judges see the gamut. Some newspapers send in their material in leather portfolios (they always want them back, darn it) full of plastic holders. Some big portfolios can display a full page at a time. And then we have the opposite. Some entries come stapled loosely or, heaven forbid, just as clippings with a paper-clipped note mentioning the category. Some come folded every bit as intricately as a piece of origami, if that's the right word for Japanese paper folding. Judges don't mind unfolding those, but they hate to try to get them back the way they came.

Somewhere between leather binders and the loosey-goosey approach lies success. Judges, seeing all that leather and plastic, sometimes feel that someone is trying to buy a blue ribbon. They get suspicious. Similarly, judges often think the people who send those casual, loose-leaf entries haven't taken the time to send something attractive because they know the entry doesn't have a winning quality. (The sponsoring organization ought to spell out how entries are to be presented. I would have them stapled into file folders generally, with some exceptions for photos and special contests that require more than just a clipping.)

So is an entry worth the effort? Sure. Oh, I would hesitate to enter a lot of industry-sponsored contests. Take hospitals, for instance. The hospital people have no evil in their hearts when they offer prizes for the best stories about hospitals. They encourage good writing about the subject—a laudable aim. The problem comes when a reporter starts writing about hospitals. If you know that a good story might win you a prize, you could let that affect you slightly. You know, to be candid about it, that a story attacking hospitals and administrators as a pack of bloodsuckers will probably fare poorly in the contest. That would not keep most of us from reporting the news, but now and then it might cause someone to hesitate. We don't need that. In addition, the appearance of honesty is as important as honesty itself. If people even think we can be bought, the damage is done.

To repeat: You should enter all state and regional contests, not to mention those of national organizations. See what other people enter, what they consider their best work. Measure them against your work, no matter what the judges have to say. Make sure you have done the best job—for your readers—that you could possibly do.

Then go collect your prizes.

# Index